Every so often you meet someone who exists out of time. Ahead of it. Behind. It doesn't matter. *"A real character"* people call them. *"A real book, that one."* You know someone like that. If you're lucky, you know a few. These extraordinary, ordinary people straddle the wobbly line between brilliance and madness, comedy and tragedy, success and failure. When they speak, it's poetry. It's in the air and then it's gone. Maybe it touches the lives of those within earshot. Maybe it's ignored altogether. Maybe it isn't even said out loud. Just a thought. A notion. A train of thoughts. **The Portrait Series** is an attempt to ride that train. It is an ongoing suite of narrative books that document and portray the stoop philosophers, sit-down comedians, and off-the-cuff bards who puncture the predictability of daily life.

D1476922

nick

is a hard-boiled, soft-hearted, retired dock worker who expounds on the meaning of life and near death from his four-room railroad flat in Long Island City, New York, where he's lived for nearly sixty years. Surrounded by cartoon and nursery rhyme characters, memorabilia, and seasonal icons of good cheer, Nicholas DeTommaso delivers a continuous stream of barbed commentary on familial duty, work, war, money, religion — and the best way to chop garlic. Undiminished by a childhood spent in a hospital, a lifetime of backbreaking work, and his share of disappointments, this irascible orator reveals a tender regard for friends and family, and a stubborn inclination for life.

nicky D.

from long island city

THE PORTRAIT SERIES

written and designed by

The Portrait Series
Nicky D. from L.I.C.

© 1995 Warren Lehrer *all rights reserved*
Object photographs by Warren Lehrer
Portrait photographs by Jim Frank and Warren Lehrer
The Lady Upstairs by Warren Lehrer and Adele Shtern
This portrait is inspired by the life of Nicholas DeTommaso.
The names of some people and institutions have been changed.
ISBN 0-941920-37-2
Library of Congress Card Number 95-5814
First printing 1995

Published by **Bay Press, Inc.**
115 West Denny Way, Seattle, Washington
9 8 1 1 9 . 4 2 0 5

The paper in this book meets the guidelines for permanence and durability
of the Committee on Production Guidelines for Book Longevity of the
Council on Library Resources. Printed in the Republic of Korea.

This book was made possible in part by a
New York State Council on the Arts Sponsored Artist Grant.

nicky D. from L.I.C.

varren lehrer

narrative portrait of
nicholas detommaso

BAY PRESS SEATTLE

with objects and pictures from the collection of

nicholas detommaso

contributing author **adele shtern**

Sixteen years ago I fancied myself a fearless street photographer barreling through the flux of human traffic in search of critical moments. I hovered around families, couples, and loners, public and private gatherings, legitimate and illegitimate commerce. In time, it dawned on me that I was more interested in what people were saying than in the way they looked. Even though I continued to snap the shutter, I stopped putting film in my camera. Eventually, I stopped carrying the camera altogether.

author's

The composition of each book in The Portrait Series is shaped by the composition of a life. The people who inspired these portraits have generously opened their lives, minds, and hearts to me over a period of at least seven years. My use of the first-person singular implies the autobiographical *I* of each subject. Their gospel, their memory, even their distortion is truth enough for me.

The monologues that make up this series are informed by the structure of supper talk, messages left on phone machines, ruminations of long walks, and reminiscences evoked by photo albums and rainy Sundays. In writing these books, I've taken liberties that a painter or photographer might take when a subject sits for a portrait. A turn of phrase, fragmentary memories, years of thought and conversation, are shaped into vignettes, short stories, confessions, diatribes, diagrams, and extended soliloquies. Many selections included in these books were developed out loud by way of readings and performance workshops.

THE PORTRAIT SERIES

note

a quartet of men

The first four books in **The Portrait Series** focus on men. Taken together, these books form a group portrait as reflective of the voices stirred within me as it is of the subjects. I offer these books to Nicky D., Claude, Brother Blue, and Charlie as gifts in return for their trust and friendship. I also offer these books to you as an opportunity to visit with, listen to, and try to understand a life, a life's perspective, the lives of four eccentric, prismatic, and resilient men.

go ahead . . .

go ahead and print it up

i got

nothin to hide

nicky D.

You don't knock. That's an insult. If it's any time between six a.m. and eleven p.m. the policy is open door. Just push. Once inside Nicky D.'s four-room railroad flat, you've entered a never-never land of cartoon characters, nursery rhymes, angels, saints, monsters, Hollywood divas, and Coca-Cola girls. Depending on the time of year, every wall and ceiling is profusely adorned with the appropriate icons of good cheer (be they goblins and skeletons, Santa Clauses and Christmas lights, turkeys and pilgrims, Easter eggs and bunnies, or birthday mementos for all the Libras in the family). Nicky D. is either in the kitchen with his sleeves rolled up, preparing the next meal to the cackle of talk radio, or he's all the way down the other end of the apartment, feet up on the coffee table, a Marlboro hanging from his lips, going through yesterday's race results in the *Daily News* with the TV tuned to a colorized movie from the forties. The aroma of Nicky D.'s famous Italian home cooking fills the dimly lit, venetian-blinded air. Stuffed chocolate samplers, candies of all stripes, and bubblegum offer themselves up to you from covered glass jars at every turn. Retirement is saying yes to all those things he couldn't do during a lifetime of hard work loading and unloading stuff from here to there. At seventy-two, with the help of daily iron pills and an inside deal with God, Nicky D. has more energy than most people I know half his age. Still, he prefers to bask (and stew) in the comfort of his own home. Before it became his own private "Shangri-la," Nicky shared this apartment in Long Island City, Queens, with his mother, three brothers, and two sisters. Before that, he lived for eight years within the mural-filled walls of the pediatric ward of an orthopedic hospital. Memories of all those years flash before him more frequently these days. Even with growing up sick, the wars, no father, very little money, and no privacy, those were good years. Today, all that really matters are his thirty-five nieces and nephews and a handful of neighbors and friends. We are the recipients of his food, his Mr. Fixit service (free of charge), and an ongoing stream of barbed commentary, argument, reminiscences, and philosophy. No need to knock. Just turn the page.

i'm

my wh

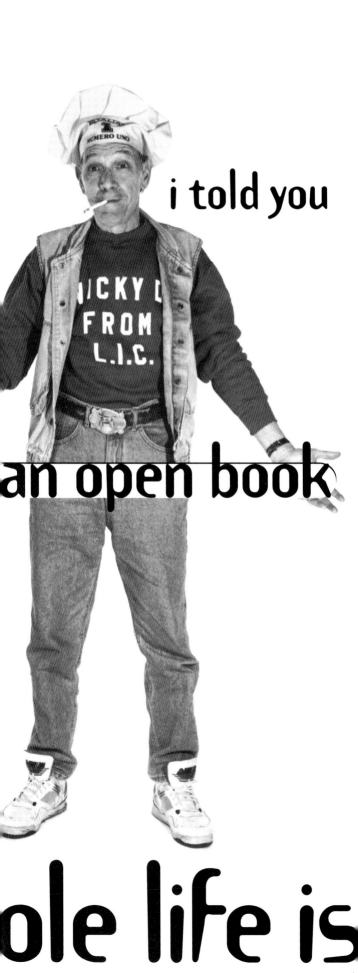

i told you

an open book

ole life is

...an open

book

NIC
FR
L.

me a book?

what d'ya wanna do make a

BEST SELLA

and make everybody commit suicide?

the people on the earth today
don't give a damn about
the things i got to say
who the fuck cares about nicky d.?

if it's part of a whole set
that's even worse!
they won't wanna buy the whole set
that's bad news
they'll probably just buy
some of the other people
nobody ever heard of me
you're gonna hafta force people
to take em all
if they're allowed to choose
i'll be left standin on the bookstore shelf
people'll say
who the hell is that guy?
i never heard of him

although . . .
alotta people know me
alotta people know nicky d.
yeah
alotta people from long island city anyway
and the loading dock at 𝕿𝖍𝖊 𝕹𝖊𝖜 𝖄𝖔𝖗𝖐 𝕿𝖎𝖒𝖊𝖘
and my family
it's a pretty big family too
i got thirty-five nieces and nephews
and they all know people who know me

all i ask is if you're gonna take my picture for the cover
make sure i got my hat on to cover up my bald head
it makes me look presentable

aaah
who the hell wants to read all my crazy ideas?
what are you nuts?
all you ever wanna do is bullshit with me all the time
 i tell you alotta secrets
   i give you alotta philosophy
      what are you gonna do with all of it
          make a best sella or somethin?
                get the hell outta here

them days ●

what's real and what's not

i'm six years old

orthopedic hospital

layin in my bed

i start to float

i float up over my bed

lookin down

i see all the other kids in the ward

i float under my bed

still in midair

not touchin the floor or nothin

i turn my head

and i'm face to face with

the bengal tiger

my whole early life i spent livin in hospitals
(ages four to twelve)
before that it's hard to remember
all i know is i was a bad boy
i was curious about everything
i was curious about windows
so i'd open em up
and fall out

      i

      fell

      out

      alotta

      windows

   i fell down stairs

   i fell outta cribs

  i fell all over the place
i broke alotta bones
doctors were always tryin to patch me up
until one time i injured my back so bad
my spine got infected
my whole body filled up with pus
they couldn't figure out what to do with me
so they took me to the hospital
and i stayed there for **eight years!**

it turned out i had osteomyelitis
(which is like tuberculosis of the bone)
they had to remove my third lumbar vertebra
and fuse the spine together
otherwise i would've crumbled up into nothin
they couldn't just do a fuse job on me like that
it took alotta years of figurin out what the problem was
tryin this and tryin that
cuttin me up
then stitchin me back together again
one surgery after the next
they even cut into me from the side one time
to get all that stuff out
i was like the scarecrow in the wizard of oz
(remember how they took him apart
and put him back together again?
that's what it was like)

what's real and what's not

it took years and years of surgery and recuperation
till i was a whole person again
then they shipped me out to another hospital
for a coupla years for rehabilitation

that was my childhood!

the orthopedic hospital i was in
had this **humongous ward** just for kids
the ceiling must've been twenty feet high
that's how big that ward was
and all around the walls were murals of
nursery rhymes and fairy tales
painted from floor to ceiling
one side of the ward was jack'n the beanstalk
on another wall alice was walking through the looking glass
there was the king of hearts and the rabbit
and humpty-dumpty
and as you came around the corner
you came to the bengal tiger who was always
chasin after little black sambo
all he wanted was to eat that brown thing
he chased him around this palm tree
he kept chasin after him
till the bengal tiger ran so fast around that palm tree
he turned into a heap of butter

nowadays the n. double a.c.p. and all them organizations
are claimin bias and discrimination
and bitchin about every friggin thing
so they chuck all them stories i growed up with
they're even tryin to chuck alotta the old movies
with colored maids and butlers and all of that
for me
growin up with them pictures on the walls
black sambo and the bengal tiger
little miss muffet and the three little pigs
they were magical creatures to me

what did i know about discrimination?

i was a sick little kid growin up in a hospital ward
those walls were my way out to happyland

i didn't even know about home
and brothers and sisters and stuff till i was twelve
i never saw my brothers
i only saw my father maybe twice in my life
the only one who ever came to visit me was my mother
maybe my grandmother came once or twice
but other than that
those creatures up on the walls were like my family

what fuckin agony and stuff i went through
f'get about it
today operations are a snap
five to ten minutes
twenty minutes

zip
zap

and you're outta there
hardly any bleeding
hardly any pain at all
in them days they had nothin!
they'd put you out with ether
work on you with nothin but scalpels
gauzes and sutures
that's it!
they didn't even have penicillin
all they had was a pile of sulfur
they'd go in there and pour the sulfur right on the wound
then put you in the recovery room to lay there
like a wet sock for about six or seven hours
before the ether wore off
that's what you looked like: a limp wet sock
and when you finally came to
all you could do is throw your guts up for a coupla hours
miserable!

this one time
(i already been through six or seven operations by then)
they cut me up
took me all apart
and stitched me back together again

then after i laid there like a wet sock for six hours
and threw up all over the recovery room
the nurses wheeled me back to the ward
lifted me onto my bed and left

they must've given me alotta that ether
cause i still could hardly open my eyes
i was half awake and half asleep
even though it was the middle of the day
the room was gettin darker and darker
there was a thunder and lightning storm goin on outside
i remember lookin straight up
and all i could see was little black sambo
he was up there runnin

what's real and what's not

he was runnin as fast as he could
i knew he was runnin from the bengal tiger
that's why i started gettin panicky
i was petrified that the tiger was loose in the ward
my fear of tigers was overwhelming
i must've absorbed too much of the murals
and the fairy tales
i believed those things so much
i could hear the panting breath of the tiger
somewhere in the room

ghhhrrrrrrr
ghhhrrrrrrrrrrr
ghhhrrrrrrrr
ghhhrrrrrrrrrrrrrr

i could hear it breathin

ghhhrrrrrrr
ghhhrrrrrrrrrrr
ghhhrrrrrrrrrrr

but i couldn't see it
i thought maybe the tiger was under my bed
maybe it crawled in between my sheets
to this day i don't know if it was cause
i wanted to jump outta my bed
but had no way of movin
or if it was cause of the ether
or what it was
but at that moment

for the first time in my life i just floated right .

. outta my body

i floated up over the bedposts
past the seven dwarfs
peter rabbit
the pied piper
and the little old lady
who lived in the shoe
i looked down and saw
all the other kids in the ward
i saw myself down on my bed
i floated from tree to tree
i floated all around till
i caught sight of little black sambo
he was runnin faster than ever
which meant that the tiger
wasn't very far behind

the next thing i know
i'm not above my bed
i'm under my bed
in some kind of suspended animation
not touchin the floor
not touchin the bed
i wasn't touchin nothin!

i turned my head and saw the tiger
   the bengal tiger was right there
      starin at me
         with his salivating fangs

i screamed

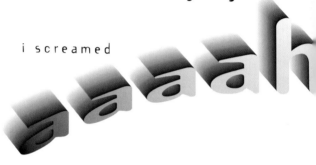

the nurses shook me
they told me i was havin a nightmare
i didn't believe em
even though i was just six years old
i knew it wasn't just a dream
i knew i actually entered some other world
a world where i could float in midair
where everyday people mix in with
cartoon creatures and fairies and ferocious animals

look
you can go ahead and think whatever you want
i know what most people think
the doctors and nurses
everybody said to me
oh nicky you were only dreaming
it was just a bad dream
but i know what happened
i know i left my body
and took off into some other dimension
you can make up all kinds of reasons why it couldn't be
you can call it confusion delusion illusion
whatever high priced words you wanna use
i know what happened to me
and **nobody's** more of an expert
on what happened to me than me
after livin seventy-two years
and bein through all i been through
i consider myself just as much of an authority
as anybody else on this earth
when it comes to knowin
what's real and what's not

dr. hibbs

after all them operations i had year after year
nothin they were doin to me was workin
all i was gettin was worse and worse and worse
till finally someone sent up a message that said

LITTLE NICHOLAS DETOMMASO
NEEDS SOME FIXIN UP

BAD!

so

they

sent

down

dr. hibbs

straight

from

heaven

he was an angel
he came down to earth just to give me a second chance
it was a miracle what he done to me!

in them days fuse jobs were big deal operations
it was a very primitive procedure
he actually had to use silver nitrate
to fuse the vertebrae together
that's the same stuff they use to melt lead
(no wonder my spine is fused together like stone)

the job he did on me today they still can't do!
with all the laser beams and high-powered painkillers
and radiation and technology
back then it was **cut**

cut

    grind

      grind

    solder

      solder

    stitch

      stitch

  scream

      scream

    pray

      pray

and see what happens

dr. hibbs had a comforting smile and a magic touch
i looked up to him like he was a godsend
he did such a beautiful job on my spine
he fixed me up good for life
i could tell cause they told me

    well nicky
    we think dr. hibbs
    put you back together again
    once and for all

i could feel i was gettin better
then a coupla days after the operation
the nurse came in and said

    nicky
    i'm sorry to have to tell you this
    but dr. hibbs is dead
    he passed away this afternoon

i remember lookin up at the nurse
(it was the middle of the day)
the moment she told me that
the whole sky turned yellow

i mean yellow!
like the yellow pages

dr. hibbs

i could see out all the windows
everything turned yellow in all directions
and then it started to rain
and then it poured
bolts of lightning crashed every which way
the whole friggin city shook with thunder
i thought the whole world was shakin

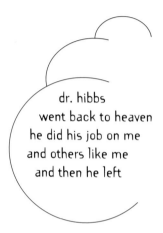

dr. hibbs
went back to heaven
he did his job on me
and others like me
and then he left

within a year i finally got outta the hospital
even though i still hadta go back for
physical therapy every day

as much as i felt at home bein in that hospital
it was also kinda creepy going back there every day
dr. hibbs was gone
most of the other kids i knew had either croaked
were transferred or let loose like me

after a while i only hadta go once a month
then a few months later they released me from
the outpatient program altogether
which meant i only hadta go back to the hospital
once a year

for five years in a row
once a year i'd go up to the orthopedic hospital
a nurse would bring me into this big big room
it was like a big hall or a ballroom
i couldn't exactly tell what kinda room it was
cause it was always so dark in there
all i could really tell for sure
was that it was very very fancy
cause the floors were made of marble
the first time i was in there i thought
what the hell is this?
get me outta here!

all kinds of scientists from all over the country
men
women
doctors
researchers
all the hotshot people in orthopedic medicine
would sit around in a big circle
the only light in the whole room
was a spotlight that aimed down from the ceiling
right to the middle of that circle

that's
where
they'd
put
me
stripped
naked
from
head
to
toe
naked!

they'd say
stand right in the middle

then they'd say
now nicky
try to touch your toes
. . . .
i'd touch my toes
. . . .
i could hear them takin notes!
now try to lean backwards
. . . .
i'd lean backwards
. . . .
i'd hear them goin
uh huh mmmmmmmmm
mmmmmmmmm uh huh
now bend from left to right
. . . .
now put your hands together like this
. . . .
now lift your shoulders

dr. hibbs

now try to jump forwards
. . . .

backwards
. . . .

mmmmmmmm wow
can you hop?
. . . .

on your right foot?
. . . .

on your left?
. . . .

now do this
. . . .

now do that
. . . .

i did everything they asked
it was like a one-ring circus
and i was the only act
i could see the faces of all the doctors gawkin at me
   mmmm mmmm
   ooooh interesting
   fascinating
   mmmmmmmm look at that

they were so amazed what this dr. hibbs had done
they'd stand up and inspect me
like i was some kind of an animal
they'd poke at me
they'd actually touch me
   mmmm mmmm
   wow! look at that

they put their fingers in the hole in my back
   mmmm mmmmm
   amazing!

they'd scratch down all their observations
and whisper to each other
all the while i could hear them whisperin
   ooh wow
   how the hell did he do that?
   unbelievable

i was supposed to be all hunchbacked
or crippled
or dead
or somethin
and here i was jumpin around like a kangaroo!

i went through those inspections every year for five years!
when the fifth year came around i finally said

when are you gonna
stop this shit?
leave me alone already
i'm seventeen years old
c'mon now
you gotta stop this already

the head doctor said
> *well mr. detommaso*
> *we're still trying to figure out*
> *exactly how dr. hibbs did that*
> *spinal fusion job of yours*

finally i looked at him and said
nah nah nah
it's been five years of this now
fuck this shit!

i never came back
but they got what they wanted
they got it all down
cause it was an experimental first for them days
  me and dr. hibbs
    we're down in history
        we're in the history books together
            me and him
                we're history

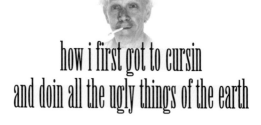

how i first got to cursin
and doin all the ugly things of the earth

i didn't even know what the word <u>Fuck</u> meant

growin up in the orthopedic hospital
i led a pretty sheltered life
still i couldn't help but hear the kids out the window
on fifty-ninth street playin in the gutter
sayin Fuck this
       Fuck that
        Fuck
          Fuck
       Fuck
    Fuck
  Fuck
i had no idea what that word meant

one afternoon the doctors and nurses wheeled me into
the room where they changed my dressing
they rolled me onto my stomach
(like they always did during a post-op period)
took the bandages off
poured rubbing alcohol on a piece of cotton
and washed all around the wound
i screamed and kicked and cried like i usually did
tears shot down my cheeks
it was a typical afternoon nightmare session
only this time
outta nowhere
in between all the hollerin
i came out with the word

Fuck

i actually said the word

Fuck

and right after i said that word

Fuck

the doctor raised his hand over his head
and
　　brought
　　　　it
　　　　　　right
　　　　　　　　down
　　　　　　　　　　on
　　　　　　　　　　　my
　　　　　　　　　　　　tush

eek

i thought to myself
jeez
i must've said a really bad word

when i found out what it meant
i couldn't believe it
i couldn't believe i actually said a thing like that

i never cursed again for as long as i was in that hospital
the way they brought me up in there
they brought me up to be like a perfect specimen
like an android
i had no reason to curse or get upset
with the things of the earth
i was protected from all that
we were completely isolated
from the outside world
all the kids were happy
growin up in the hospital

we believed in santa claus
every christmas
we'd sit on santa's lap
he'd give us presents
the easter bunny
came around every easter
if you lost a tooth
the tooth fairy came around
we had ghosts and goblins
on halloween
pumpkin lanterns
pilgrims and indians
on thanksgiving
all them things were real to me

how i first got to cursin . . .

growin up in a pediatric ward was a great education
whatever they told me i absorbed
they taught me everything
we had the best teachers
they gave us books and pencils and lessons in reading
writing
mathematics
everything!
alotta people don't believe me when i tell em
what a good upbringing i had in the hospital

but then when i was twelve years old
i finally got discharged
for the first time in eight years i got to go home
to live with my mother and brothers and sisters
after spending my whole early life on the operating table
i finally came home to live in a house
(not this house
but the one around the corner
same thing as this
a four-room railroad flat straight through)
it was like movin to another planet

i was a scared scrawny little faggot kid
takin a crash course on how to survive in a new world:

the street

just walkin around was a whole new experience
crossin the street
bein in the school yard with other kids
goin to school for the first time in my life
i was terrified
i wasn't prepared for the ugliness
i wasn't prepared for the meanness in the outside world
i wasn't streetwise
not at all
kids started robbin my toys
they took my little white milk truck
with the little man and all the little bottles
i treasured that milk truck!
they took my little cars and my little train set
i even had a little toy rifle
with a cork in the end that would go **pop**
they took that
life was a struggle from the second i got out
kids in the neighborhood beat on me
they used all kinds of curse words against me
i never even heard of some of those words

after a few weeks i figured out i had to get in good
with the other kids
so i started cursin and swearin just to blend in
i learnt how to protect myself
after all them years they educated me in the hospital
after all them years of goodness
within a coupla weeks
i turned into a little monster

my own brothers
treated me like a stranger
the second i walked in the door
it was instant combat

two of them ganged up on me one day
tony punched my face in
while vinny held my legs down
they tied my arms and legs to the bed
and left me there
till my mother came home and found me

i tasted revenge for the first time in my life
they made a **frankenstein** outta me

a few days after they tied me up
i took out my toy rifle
threw out the cork
opened the door of the stove
(in them days we had a belly stove to keep warm)
i shoved the barrel of the gun into the white coals
and waited till it got red-hot
then i took it outta the coals
i went into the back room and asked my brother
hey vinny
you wanna play with my gun?

yeah

you can play with my gun
here
i handed him the gun by the barrel
he grabbed at it and the gun stuck to his hand
and burnt the shit out of it

i did a few things like that to all three of my brothers
they didn't bother with me after that
i learnt fast
cause i hadta survive

how i first got to cursin . . .

more than just survive
there's somethin in me that makes me
wanna excel at whatever i do
wherever i am i pick up on the situation
i absorb knowledge very quickly

ST. MARY'S SCHOOL
LONG ISLAND CITY N. Y.

saint mary's school didn't know where to put me
after i got outta the hospital
they figured i didn't know anything
so at first they put me in 2a
within a week they skipped me to 4a
after a few months they skipped me
all the way to 6 somethin
they had no idea how good an education
i got in the hospital
i was already programmed!
i didn't hafta study
i knew all the stuff the nuns were talkin about
i got medals every single term
i got the highest marks in the class

99
98
100

even in music i got like an **86**
i picked up a harmonica and figured out how to play it

even though i was becomin a tough guy out on the street
i still did well in school
whatever was put in front of me
whether it was stealin apples on the corner
or learnin my times tables
i was good at it

i got to be so far ahead of the rest of my class
the teachers got disgusted with me
they didn't want me to learn no more
when i got to the higher grades
they gave me all kinds of errands to do

even the principal (the head nun)
used to say

nicholas
go down to the boiler room
for me and help mr. daily

i spent a coupla hours a week shovelin coal in the boiler
takin the ashes out
me and mr. daily were like two coal miners
we took lunch breaks together
we'd eat these guinea meatball heroes
and drink pepsi cola
i was hardly ever in class!

alotta times if the teacher hadta leave the room
she'd say

nicholas
please come up and
take care of the class for me

so i'd take care of the class
hand out papers
give out tests
whatever it was she wanted
i did it

when i took the regents exams and the finals
at the end of the year
i didn't do a thing

zip
zip
zip
zip

90s
100s

every year at the last assembly
the principal would call me and irene duzer up to the stage
to give us the highest honors
the two of us would win every year
every year it was me and irene
me and irene

but then i started gettin disgusted with school
by the time i got to ninth grade i was sick of it!
i said
ahhhh
to hell with all this!

how i first got to cursin . . .

whatever good ways i had left
were almost completely gone
i got in with a bad crowd
i skipped classes to smoke cigarettes out on the street
i did all kinds of bad things
we robbed coal off of trains
(me and one of my new buddies)
we'd go down to the railroad at night with burlap bags
climb up on the train
fill the bags up with coal
climb down
then go around the neighborhood sellin coal to people
fifty cents for a hundred-pound sack
eighty or ninety pounds would keep a whole block
nice and warm

one time i was makin the rounds along jackson avenue
with a sack of coal on my back
goin down the block knockin on doors
makin some money
till i knocked on this one door
and guess who opens it?

sister o'donnell

(one of the teachers at saint mary's school)
i was so shocked
i dropped the sack right on her doorstep
and tore outta there faster than a jackrabbit
habada
   habada
      habada
         habada

i didn't care no more about school
i started to get D's in etiquette and hygiene
and stuff like that
i joined up with a gang called the black knights

eventually i became better than all them other fucks
  • i ran faster
  • caught the most balls
  • fought harder
  • swore dirtier
  • drank more
  • played kick the can better
    than every one of them punks

i could climb too
i was like a wild monkey
i started out climbin trees
from there i went on to roofs
and then daredevil stunts
i became a demon
one time i hitched behind a car goin through a dirt road
with potholes every two feet
i slipped off the back of it
and my shirt got caught on the bumper
that car dragged me for **a whole block**
when i got to the corner i just let go
i was bleedin from the top of my head
to the bottom of my toes

when i came home my mother clobbered me
my clothes were ripped to shreds
i didn't give a shit
i went right back out and tried somethin else
i jumped on top of a trolley car up on vernon avenue
hitched a ride all the way to astoria park
we were scugnizzios!
we were crazy bastards!
to get to central park at night
we'd climb up the queensboro bridge
then walk across on the catwalk doin handstands!
we were fearless
we'd pick up cigarette butts off the street
light em and smoke em
who cared what the hell people had
tuberculosis
pneumonia
leprosy
pick up a pretzel out of the gutter
blow off the ants and eat it!

i came outta the hospital a blonde-haired kid
wearin short boy scout pants
holdin a book under my arm
and the fear of god over my head
within eight months
my hair turned brown
i started to sweat
i was filthy
i **learnt** about all the ugly things of the earth
i started **doin** the ugly things of the earth
i **became** one of the ugly things of the earth

the civilian conservation corps

after i graduated from saint mary's school
by the skin of my teeth
i knew i didn't wanna go to high school
but then i got my mind set on learnin electronics
so i went to queens vocational and took up radio
that was my love – **radio**
them days very few people had radios
they were so expensive
but i knew there'd come a day
everybody would have a radio in their house
and they'd need fixin
so i learnt all about electronics
i built my own radio from scratch
it was easy for me and i liked it
my brother sal went to queens vocational too
he took up auto mechanics
and he don't even know how to change a fuckin spark plug
shows you how phony them schools were

while i was at queens vocational
the germans marched into poland
which screwed up the depression even worse
so i hadta quit school and look for work
help put food on the table
i signed up with the c.c.c.
the united states army **1940**
Civilian Conservation
Corps

those
were
my
happy
days
workin
up
near
the
canadian border
once you volunteered
they could send you anywhere
you could go north south
east or west

north
west — or — east
south

i happened to go north
even though i was dressed to go south
they shipped me up to a little town just north of syracuse
they classified me as a **forestry axman**

we chopped down trees

we knocked ourselves out
but we had fun doin it
our job was to climb up these mountain hills
chop down all the dirty diseased trees
haul em back down to chenango valley
then we'd take off our dirty uniforms

and

stand

in

line

to

walk

through

the

showers

pickin

wood

ticks

off

each

other's

backs

them little wood tick shits were rampant up there
they'd give you rocky mountain spotted fever
which was a deadly disease back then
to get em off you had to strike a match
hold it over the skin
and wait for them to **pop** right off

the civilian conservation corps

cause if you didn't get em right away
they'd bore straight in
so we did that ritual every day
then we'd go into syracuse for r & r on the weekend
they used to lock up the town
cause the townies didn't want us in there
every place closed soon as they seen the army truck
comin in with the **C.C.C.** guys in their green uniforms
the only place that would let us in was the poolroom
so we played alotta pool
we met girls in there
we drank beer
it was alotta fun

but then . . .
(cause the war was
spreadin out all over europe)
they wanted to convert that camp
into a military post
**throw away the shovels and axes
and give the guys guns**
i figured if we were goin to join the war
i didn't wanna be stuck in chenango county new york
i wanted to be where the action was!
so i went over the hill (which means a.w.o.l.)
i put my trunk on my back
and hitched all the way back to the city
you should've seen me standin there
in the middle of times square
with my foot locker on my shoulder
wearin my green uniform
green arctic boots
green pants
green hood
green everything
people were lookin at me like i was the man from mars
with that big patch on my arm — **C.C.C.**

those were the best of days!

service

all i wanted to do was fly them fighter planes
that was my life ambition
to join the air force and fight for my country
see the world
i set my heart on it
i had such a passion for flyin

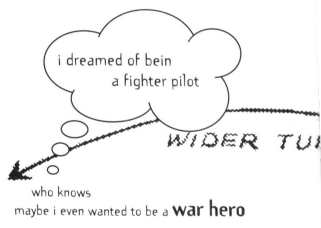

i dreamed of bein
a fighter pilot

WIDER TUR

who knows
maybe i even wanted to be a **war hero**

TIGHT
TURN

ALLIE

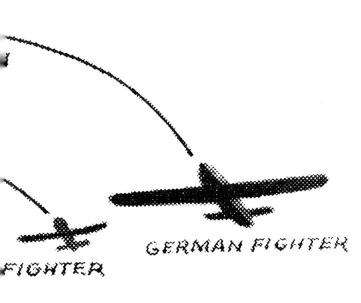

GERMAN FIGHTER

FIGHTER

so i went to volunteer downtown
at the air force recruitment office
i filled out all the forms
i did whatever they told me
the sergeant said
you might go to training at these places
you might be on duty over here
or over there

everything was goin smooth till they gave me a checkup
soon as they saw the hole in my back
they said
no
we can't use you in the air corps

service

so i went over to the marines
filled out all the forms
then they sent me in for a checkup with the doctor
and he kicked me right outta there

the navy i didn't care for
cause i never cared too much for water

before you know it
the fuckin army grabbed me
i was in the first draft in long island city
it was on the front page of the *long island star*

39 MEN FROM THE FIRST QUEENS DRAFT GROUP HEAD FOR THE SUBWAY TO START A TRIP THAT MAY LEAD TO 21 MONTH HITCHES IN THE ARMY

he
UNS
NAVY

me and thirty-eight other guys from long island city
took the train to grand central
then they threw us in a bus
and took us over to new jersey

camp dix

there were all these canvas tents and all these shacks
i went into one shack and filled out all the forms
then i went into this other long shack
where everyone got examined

they lined us all up
we're all walkin along in the buff
they're checkin me for hernias
they're lookin in my throat
they're checkin out my teeth
every friggin place i got a hole
they looked inside it

bend over

· · · · · · · · · · ·

say aahhhhh

service

hold your breath
. . . .

touch your toes
. . . .

look straight at the light
. . . .

listen for the tone
. . . .

they touch me here
. . . .

they touch me there
. . . .

they touch me all over!
. . . .

then i go over to the next shack
(it was like a conveyor belt)
the doctor's standin behind me
and i hear him say

        oh
        um
        what uh
        what's that?

now
if you never seen the hole in my back
the first time you see it
it can get you to do the fuckin lindy!

(the skin
towards the middle
of nicky's spine is
tightly pinched into
a one-inch black
vortex)

so i told the doctor
when i was a kid i had osteomyelitis
in the third lumbar vertebra
they did a miracle fuse job on me
since then i never had a backache once
i been loadin ships
packin trucks
haulin cargo
everything!

'n i told that army doctor
i'm any less nervous about the hole in my back
t me over to another shack

to see the commanding officer
the commanding officer looks at my papers
and he looks at my back and says
**well nicholas detommaso
you know we'd like to have you in the army**

i say
yeah i'd like to go in the army too

he says
well it requires your signature on this form here

i say
what is it?

so he says
**it's only for . . .
just in case you're over in france or england
or italy or someplace like that
wherever we'd be shippin you
and if somethin was to happen
to that back of yours
the army's not responsible**

so i say to the commander
first of all commander
if i don't sign this here document
then what?

he says
**then we gotta send you back home
and classify you 4f**

so i say
can't you take me the way i am?
i mean suppose i did go over to france
or england or italy or someplace
and (god forbid) somethin
did happen to my back

the commander says
then uncle sam would have no responsibility

at which point i stand up and say
well listen
if you want me
then tear that piece of paper up
and take me!

service

the commanding officer looked down
at the piece of paper
he looked back up at me
he reached into his pocket
took out a nickel and said
**here's some money for the train
go home kid**

i said

**well that's alright with me
uncle sam grabbed my
three brothers
he grabbed my father
in the first fuckin war
sent him home with no lungs
he's gone
so now i gotta be the father
i gotta take care of
my mother and
my two baby sisters**

and that's what i did
all through the war
i took care of the home front
while my three brothers were fightin for uncle sam
tony on the heavy cruiser fightin the coral sea battles
sal on the minesweeper (invasion of normandy) and
vinny fightin hand-to-hand combat in the argonne forest
i went to work every day on the docks of new york
fuck uncle sam
i tried to fight for my country
but they wouldn't let me
so i did the best thing i could've done
i stayed home and took care of my family
   that's what i did for my country
      i took care of my family
         they needed me
            i took care of them
               and i'm proud of it

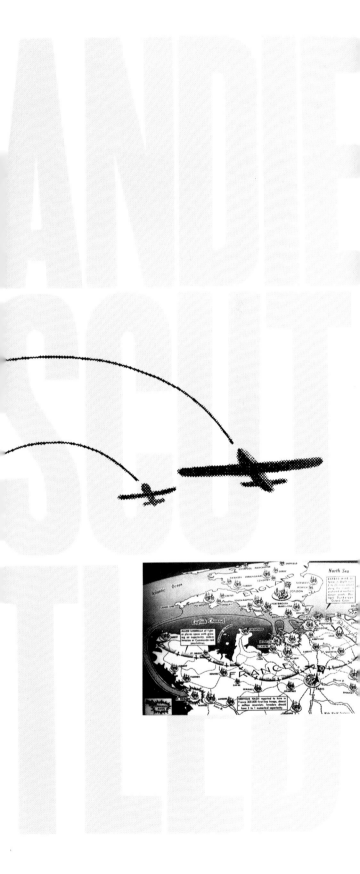

longshoreman

after bein turned down by the air force
the marines and the army
i hadta come to terms with findin civilian work
so i got a job over at walde's zipper factory
as a die setter
(today they'd pay you alotta money for that job
that's a big deal position)
in them days i was gettin forty-five cents an hour
which was good money back then
you could bring home twenty dollars a week
support the family for a whole month
and have pocket change to spare
but then my uncle talked to me about
workin as a longshoreman

for the next four years
i worked with the mafia
(the ambrosini brothers)
as a longshoreman
we worked the docks in manhattan
south brooklyn
staten island
all the piers
everywhere there was water and a dock to hitch a boat to
we worked

first thing in the morning
i'd go right into the hold of the ship
cause my uncle had pull with all the hatch bosses

when i first started out i hadta wait around on this big line
in a circle like everybody else
the hatch boss'd stand in the middle and point ☞ you
you
you
you
you
you

i did that every day till i got in with a steady gang
and when you're in a steady gang
you just go to work every day
you don't hafta stand around waitin to get picked

i liked the security of bein in with the gang
but i also felt sorry for all them other guys
havin to stand around in the rain and snow

one night we got called in for a job on pier 17
(at the foot of jeralemon street in brooklyn)
we took the **GG** train and got off at fulton street
then we hadta take a long walk
all the way down to the pier
we're hikin down
hikin down
hikin down to the docks
and just as we're about to approach the dock
i hear somethin like a firecracker or an explosion

i see the other guys divin under cars
i'm thinkin **holy shit**

that's gunfire!

so i dive under the nearest car
and watch all these bullets ricochet every which way
my heart's poundin a mile a minute
i'm scared outta my mind
the bullets are goin

zing
zang
zing

zing
zing zang

zing

zing
zing

they're flyin all over the place

when the commotion finally dies down
i check to see if the coast is clear
then i slip out from under the car thinkin
**forget about workin tonight
i'm goin back home!**

the next day i found out it was the ambrosini brothers
blowin each other up

**they were fightin each other
for control of the pier
those friggin guys
were unbelievable!**

longshoreman

it wasn't until a coupla years later
that they finally got anthony ambrosini
he was gettin a shave in a barbershop
down on mulberry street when
one of his brother's boys clipped him with a machine gun
right in the middle of the day

New York, Monday, December 8, 1941*

JAPS BOMB HAWAII
DECLARE WAR ON U.S. AND BRITAIN

then the japs did their thing at pearl harbor
and america got into the war

that's when everything changed
i kept workin for the ambrosini brothers
but i never came home
there was so much work loadin up liberty ships
we'd load a ship up to the hilt
then another ship would come in
we'd load that up
i'd eat with the navy crews
then crash for the night on whatever ship we were loadin
hang out with the sailors
another ship would come in
we'd load that up
i only came home to say hello
and put some money on the table
then i'd run right back to the docks

we'd load them big white monster ships up with supplies

ship em out to russia
england
france
wherever they needed supplies for the war

there's five hatches on a liberty ship
i was assigned to number three
me and my gang had to make sure that we loaded
the hatch properly and all the way up
whether it was flour
coffee
sugar
general cargo
it didn't matter
we had locomotives lashed on deck
p-38 fighter planes on deck too (parts and everything)
we'd lash em right on there

in the middle of the winter the decks were all icy
if you took a flop you'd go slidin down the deck
and crash right into a piece of cargo
what alotta fun!

one day i took my gloves off
everything was so frozen
my hand stuck to one of them iron turnbuckles
my whole hand got stuck!
a bunch of guys had to come and pull me off it
all my skin came off
(ever touch anything like dry ice?
it sticks to your flesh and won't come off)

ow!

we also helped the navy crews mount five-inch guns
on the bow and the stern of the liberty ships

then they'd all meet out in the atlantic and form convoys
the german subs sat there waitin for em
right off of coney island
they'd follow em out to sea and then

BOOM

BOOM

BOOM

the germans had a field day
they sunk alotta them ships we loaded
the nimitz and all them submarines
thousands of tons of stuff we loaded onto them ships

gone

we'd load up a ship

BOOM

the nazi subs would sink it

another ship'd come in
we'd load that up

BOOM

they'd sink it

BOOM

we'd wait for another one
load it up
send it out

BOOM

they sunk plenty of them liberty ships we loaded
the german subs moved in wolf packs
admiral dönitz had em takin potshots

ding

ding

ding

ding

the japs too
came right up on the shores of
long island with them one-man submarines
they sent spies in with em
they did alotta that on the west coast too
verybody thought the war
s just goin on overseas

hit!
e goin on right here!

they kept that a big secret from the people
the enemy was too far away to bomb us
but they spied and prowled
and ganged up on our ships

if a world war like that was to happen today
we wouldn't be safe here
not in greenpoint
not in times square
this is ground zero man!
all they hafta do today is press a button
and you can kiss the empire state building good-bye

remember the buzz bombs hitler threw onto london
they sent up these rockets
filled with gasoline and dynamite
and when they ran outta gas
they'd just fall right down
rrrrrrrruhhh

BOOM

rrrrrrrruhhh

BOOM

rrrrrrrruhhh

BOOM

the people could hear em comin
  they made an ugly sound like a buzz
    they'd go **rrrrrrrrrrrrrrrrrrruuhhhh**
     and as soon as that sound stopped
      everybody'd run for cover
       cause the buzz bombs would drop straight down

   BOOM

    blow up a full square block
              (the germans were only guessin where
              the bombs would run outta gas)
              today you can shoot off
              a long-range missile
              and have it drop on a dime

     BOOM

longshoreman

i might've been stuck in long island city
but i was in the middle of the war effort
i was part of it
and that made me happy
i worked around the clock
i took home $147 a week
(that's like $800 or $900 a week today)
my family had enough food on the table
plus i had alotta friends
i was hangin around with sailors from all over the country
all over the world!
the only bad thing was
as soon as i'd get to know a bunch of guys
i'd hafta say **so long** and send em out to sea
knowin that many of em would never make it
that was the tough part

after the war ended
i worked as a presser in a tailor shop
it was okay work
the money was alright
the people were nice
it was quiet
i was a good presser
but . . .
  well . . .
    i guess it wasn't half as much fun
       as bein a longshoreman
           with the mafia during the war

on marriage

i'm a loner!
what can i tell you?
marriage never was meant for me
i stuck with my mother
she was the only lady i ever lived with

except for my one big mistake in 1950

we all had girlfriends in them days
every guy had his own girlfriend
i courted mine for seven friggin years
childhood sweethearts
that's what they called it
almost eighty percent of the guys
married their neighborhood girls
alotta times the girl'd get pregnant
and you hadta marry em
plenty of shotguns in them days
but then we got into the war
and alotta the guys went overseas
they married japs
they married whatever friggin country they were in
they made puppies over there
then they came back and married the girls back here
everything was all screwed up
people started
gettin married like crazy!
in time all my brothers got married
tony got married
sal got married
vinny got married

that was the thing
gettin married

when ya gettin married?
i'm gettin married
married married
did ya hear so'n so's gettin married to so'n so
and what's his face is marryin what's her name?

all of a sudden everyone in the family was married
all my friends left the neighborhood to get married

married married married
when ya gettin married?

so after seven years of courtin this girl i say to her
we're gonna get married

she had just moved up to utica new york
to live with her sister
cause her sister married this guy from utica
so i filled up my tank with gas
i had a '39 plymouth
with the swordfish ornament on the hood
and i'll never forget — i got the flu
or a really bad virus or somethin
i was runnin a fever (a hundred and two)
but still i drove all the freakin way up to utica
they gave us the veterans hall for the reception
but the ceremony was in the syrian orthodox church
just cause my childhood sweetheart moved up to utica
to be near her sister who married a syrian
all of a sudden
i'm havin a friggin roman catholic syrian orthodox wedding
with all the rigmarole
and i don't go for that shit
but they're all syrians up there in utica

so there i am
with the stain glass and the golden robes
and drinkin wine outta silver goblets
and the father's up there at the pulpit with the big book
and all he wants to do is read that book
for hours and hours
meanwhile i'm sweatin bullets
my temperature is goin up and up
i can feel in the pit of my stomach
somethin's wrong
somethin doesn't feel right about the whole thing
there's a light comin through the stain glass windows
way up high
it's blindin me

on marriage

i start thinkin

maybe god's tryin to tell me somethin
maybe the lord almighty's tellin me
he don't want me to get married

cause first of all he gives me the flu

he was givin me a warnin with that — see?

but i was confused

he was probably tryin to warn me for a long time

but it was too late to be changin my mind

in the middle of the wedding ceremony

so i figure

this is it!
there's no gettin outta this one now

i'm standin at the altar

the father's mumblin somethin from the big book

i don't know what he's sayin cause i can't hear nothin

i'm gettin weaker and weaker

the father says to me

you have to drink a little more wine

i sip the wine

then they run this big white sheet from the street

all the way down the aisle of the church

next thing i know

the father's puttin a crown of thorns on my head

(like they did to christ

right before they nailed him to the cross)

i don't know what they're gonna do to me next

the father comes at me again with the chalice in his hands

i take another sip of wine and the room starts spinnin

i can see they're goin through the whole rigmarole

it's all a big blur to me

i start whisperin

> c'mon father
>
> hurry it up
>
> hurry it up
>
> let's just get it over with
>
> please
>
> i feel weak
>
> i feel faint

the father says

okay
that's alright my son
we'll stop the ceremony

the father stops the ceremony and tells me

sit down my son

so i sit down and put my head between my knees
when i close my eyes
i feel the blood rush up into my head
everything's spinnin and twirlin
i'm hearin voices

did ya hear so'n so's

gettin married to what's his name?

married guess who's gettin married?

married

married your brother's gettin married?

married **married** **married**

married

married

after a while i feel a little bit better
so we continue with the ceremony
the priest gets back to his mumblin
i'm sippin the wine
i'm sippin the wine
and outta nowhere
i start hearin a voice inside my head
it's my guardian angel tryin to tell me somethin
my guardian angel is whisperin in my ear

don't do this

don't do this

sure enough the marriage didn't last
six friggin weeks!

i got up one sundee morning and my wife says
drive me home to my mother
she packed her two bags of luggage
i threw em in the car
we drove over to her mother's house in total silence
i dropped the bags by the front gate
said **bye-bye**
gave her a kiss

on marriage

and zipped right outta there as fast as i could
and that was the end of that

that was forty-three years ago and i never seen her since

i really don't know what went wrong
i guess she couldn't cope with
the different hours i kept and everything
see
i was workin in the post office on a twenty-four-hour shift
you know one week 8 to 4
another 12 to 8
plus when i volunteered to be the superintendent
of the apartment building we were livin in over in astoria
she said

> *don't do that*
> *please don't do that nicky*

i took care of fifty families
hadta go down and stoke the boilers with coal
take out twenty-five or thirty garbage cans
filled with ashes
we got a deal on the rent!
so between that and the post office
we managed to make ends meet
but she couldn't stay home alone at night
without gettin the willies
she was always nervous
she was always callin me up
but what could i do?
what could i say?
in them days you didn't need to worry like you do today
she was a nervous wreck for no good reason

the other big thing was i had problems with her family
every time i'd come home from work she'd have
her whole friggin family at the table waitin for me
so they could eat
i didn't mind it once in a while
but you know eventually i said
hey c'mon now
we're married!
i didn't marry your mother
i didn't marry your sisters
c'mon now
your brothers are always here

i hafta always make sure
to get em this and
get em that

i'm
breakin
my
ass

i married <u>you</u>
that's all i married
i just married <u>you</u>
me and <u>you</u>
<u>you</u> and me
that's all!

when she told me to take her back home to her mom
i told her

you can't do that
what the hell is this?
it can't be this way!
when i was standin
there in front of the
padre and he said

until death do you part

i said yes!

cause i told my guardian angel after she warned me

don't do this
don't do this

on marriage

i told her
i'm sorry but it's too late
all these people are here
and some of them came from very far away
and it cost alotta money
for the food and everything
and after i been courtin her for
seven friggin years
somethin's gotta happen
i'm not just gonna live with my mother
for the rest of my life
don't get me wrong
i really appreciate you lookin after me
and thanks for the advice
and the warnings and everything
but i have to go through with this thing

i told my guardian angel
i hafta make the best of the situation
that's all there is to it

i never told my wife about my conversation with the angel
but what i did say was
wait a minute here
i told you
and i told the priest
and everybody
in that church i do
do you remember that?
i said i do
you said i do
we both said i do
in front of the lord almighty
in front of all them people
we made our vows
to do this thing
we're gonna hafta
do this thing
we're married!

i went to my parish and told the priest my story
he said

well that's your cross
you have to carry it

i never gave her no divorce
cause in the eyes of the catholic church
you can't get no divorce
she's automatically ex-communicated from the church
but according to the laws of new york state
we're not married no more
how could we be?
she's gone on to have two kids by another guy since then
that's why i went down to the license bureau
a few years ago
to find out my official marital status
turns out there's a statute of limitations
thirty-five or forty years without contact and you're not
considered married in the eyes of the law

good-bye
what are you gonna do?
that's why i say

don't get married
cause as soon as you get married
love flies out the window

after mushin it up in the rumble seats
and goin to beaches and parties and dances
for seven years with the same broad
then in six weeks

boom!

(maybe if we just kept courtin
we'd still be together
who the hell knows)

carmella and tommy

that there is a picture of tommy's mother carmella
my cousin ralphy was datin her at the time
still today alotta people think
that the baby belonged to ralphy
that ralphy is tommy's real father
most people never forgave carmella neither
cause ralphy was a married man
he got blamed for that
you know in them days
when somethin like that happened
people just assumed
it wasn't like today
today they have you do gene testing
and all kinds of scientific things to prove you're the father
he might be the father
he might not be

it was like musical chairs
the boys were goin out with girls
first she's my steady
then you're his steady
then you're someone else's steady
then before you know it somebody gets married
somebody else is pregnant
another one moves out of town
**everything's happenin
at the same time!**

another thing you gotta understand is
ralphy was the clark gable in them days
he was blamed for all the babies bein born
they even tried to blame my wife's sister's baby on him too

sure — he was a big womanizer
carmella was one of ralphy's girls
everybody knew that
he had a bunch of different girls
even though he just got married to maria

i don't know what the truth is
all i know is
carmella really loved that baby!

she loved it so much
but she was too messed up to do anything about it
she didn't know how to take care of herself
how was she gonna take care of a baby?

so one day
i just come home from food shoppin with my mother
and i get a phone call

the baby's sick!

i jump in my car with my mother
drive up to the bronx
go down into the basement
where carmella was livin
the baby's layin there in the manger
i look around and i can't believe it!
there's mice and rats runnin around
the baby's coughin up a storm
the place stinks
the curtains are all closed
it's pitch-black even though
it's the middle of the day
so i scoop up the baby
and take him to our place

we were just gonna take care of him for a little while
but then not too long after
carmella all of a sudden passed away
it was tragic
they woke me up in the middle of the night
to come and identify the body
i was the first one on the scene with the police
she'd moved from her basement apartment
to an attic rattrap in flushing
with a two-burner gas stove
and i think cause the room was so small
(bein that it was a cold winter day)
she turned on both them burners to get some heat
walked over to her bed
laid down with a paperback
dozed off
and never woke up
that's the thing about them carbon monoxide burners
it's an odorless gas
it sucks out all the oxygen in the room
and takes you with it

carmella and tommy

i guess it's a pleasant way to go
cause you don't feel nothin
but i don't think that's what she wanted
even though she had plenty of reason to be despondent
i could see bein depressed in her situation
but after i seen the way she was stretched out there
on the bed with the paperback opened on her chest
that's when i came to the conclusion
that she didn't **plan** on committin suicide
in fact the first police report said that it wasn't a suicide
but they came to that conclusion for the wrong reason
they wrote down

the gas jets were off

but when i went back to the apartment to snoop around
i could see the gas jets were actually **on**
there was just no flame
(after there's no more oxygen left in the room
the flame goes out)
that's why the police first put it down as an

accident

but then for some reason they changed it to a

suicide

bein that she was catholic
we tried to convince them to turn it back into an

accident

so she could have a proper burial
at least we managed to convince the priest that it was an

accident

she had no real family of her own
so we buried her on top of my father
we even had a catholic mass and everything
cause if you're catholic and you kill yourself
you can't go to heaven
and you can't have a proper burial
this keeps alotta catholics from killin themselves
but that's no good reason not to kill yourself
i mean you should **never** kill yourself anyway
but not cause you won't go to heaven

you shouldn't kill yourself cause
you're put on this earth
for somethin
and that's what you should be doin

but with carmella
the cards she got dealt were just no damn good

so me and mom ended up raising tommy together
we took him in when he was just a newborn in 1947
and he lived with me
right up until two years
after my mother died
in 1970

then in '72 he went out on his own
i wasn't even married
and i raised this guy like
he was my own son

i got all the poison that fathers have
i thought i'd be happy
i went through the whole bit
raising that guy
i taught him how to walk
how to talk
i bought him his first set
of electric trains
i taught him how to play baseball
i took him to work with me

then uncle sam grabbed him
and took him to viet fucking nam
where he won the purple heart
he was just a little kid
so they made him a machine gunner on a personnel carrier
if you see the pictures of him
the machine gun is bigger than he is
he was just a baby

one day the personnel carrier
ran over a mine and flipped over
that's when he ruined his ear
(he was deaf for about a month after he came back)
that's when alotta the aggravation started

me and my mom bringin up this boy together
worked out pretty good for a long time
then just around that whole vietnam period

carnella and tommy

when he turned 17
          18
                    19
                         20 years old
that's when we started havin too many discrepancies
between me — tryin to keep some rules
and my mother — disagreein with me
interferin
i was the bad cop
she was very lenient with him
like one time i went in his drawer
and found a bag of marijuana
that's the same thing as grass right?
whatever it is
pot
grass
i took it
and i emptied it in the terlet
and flushed it

when he got home that night i saw him lookin around
lookin inside his drawer
all over the place
          so i said
               ## whatcha doin?
          he says
               nothin
               i say
               ## whatcha lookin for
               ## a little white cloth bag?

               yeah!

               ## i threw it in the fuckin terlet
               (he went through the roof)
               i said
               ## if you wanna hang around here
          ## you gotta smoke marlboro
     # or philip morris
   # or go fuck yourself!
my mother stepped in between us two every time
cause alotta times i wanted to throw him
right through the window
but i never really hit him
i absorbed everything
how do you think my stomach exploded?
how do you think i acquired

that friggin gastric ulcer?
From holdin back
holdin back
holdin back
holdin back
that's how i got it!

if he was my own son
i probably would've clobbered him

even though ralphy is my first cousin
he stayed away from our place
all the while tommy was growin up
he stood with all his daughters that he had
ralphy and tommy used to bump into each other
from time to time at family gatherings
but that was about it
tommy knew the rumors about ralphy bein his father
and that's what he always believed
to this day he hates his guts
he says

fuck my father
my father did this
my father did that

i never really talked to ralphy too much about it
once or twice i might've said
you think tommy is really your son?

he always said

nah
he ain't my son

to tell you the truth i don't know what ralphy thinks
all i know is tommy don't seem to be a detommaso
cause he's small like a midget
detommasos are all big
and he don't have the detommaso ways
you know
he's so self-centered and independent
we raised him with all good things
as a kid he did the things he learnt from us
but as soon as he got old enough to do his own thinkin
he reverted back to whatever origin he belongs to
that's what i think

carnella and tommy

after he got back from vietnam
i got him a job workin with me at **The New York Times**

then he met this girl and they got married
his wife's uncle was a big guy in the asbestos union
he filled tommy's head up with all nice things
come'n work with us
we'll take care of you

so he told me he wanted to quit
i said **no!**

but he took off to work with asbestos anyway
so i said
to hell with you
beat it!

then he had a little baby
and then his wife and him got a divorce
so the girl's uncle (the union guy)
did bad things to tommy for divorcin his niece
including makin sure the asbestos place dumped him

so tommy was out of a job
but he was too proud to fess up to bein wrong
till a coupla years later
when they found out asbestos was poison
he came back with his head down and apologized
i shoulda listened to ya uncle nicky

yeah okay
it's another mistake you made

so he started comin around again
like *oh yeah i remember you*
but then after a while
he got to be jealous of the lady upstairs
he complained to my sister annemarie
uncle nicky is always
hangin out with that girl upstairs

annemarie by that time was jealous too
she didn't like me minglin in with anybody other than her
so she and tommy ganged up with each other against me
cause they thought if i was payin attention to other people
i was takin somethin away from them

then after the whole fracas at philomena's wedding
he never talked to me again

that's why i think maybe he ain't a detommaso after all
cause why ain't he got some kind of compassion
or love for me after all i did for him?

maybe it's in the blood
maybe we do got different blood
me and him
maybe if they had the d.n.a. test back then
none of this would've happened
my mother never would've taken him in
if she thought he wasn't a blood relation

　　　　now he's forty-somethin
　　　　　and he don't even bother with me no more
　　　　he crossed me off his list
　　　the only thing i know about him now is
　　　after waitin nine years on a list
　　the sanitation department finally called him up
so he's workin with them now
and he's got his own co-op (or condo) in forest hills
that's all i know
i haven't seen him or heard from him
since philomena's wedding
he don't even send me birthday cards or nothin
it's a complete cutoff now
even his friends inquire
everyplace i go they bump into me
how's tommy?
how's tommy?
how's tommy?
i tell em
i don't know
i'm only his fuckin uncle
i only raised him like he was my son
if you ever contact him
tell him nicky d. is still roamin the earth

　　　　he broke my heart
　　　　he broke my fuckin belly
　　　　　not a christmas card
　　　　　nothin

those beautiful girls

i think about all those girls (in the old days)

all those beautiful girls

they don't make beautiful girls like that no more
unh uh
that's why i held on to them
at least as many as i could
the best ones i saved for myself

this here is my collection
the whole wall
those are all coca-cola girls!
don't you love those girls?

the way they used to do them coca-cola girls
with all the detail
they go back to the 1800s
they don't know how to make beautiful girls like that today
today they make everything outta plastic

in them days
they used only good materials
real aluminum
the best inks
    embossments
        beautiful!
            nothin in the modern age
                can make me happy like that
                    nothin!

there's not supposed to be
no such thing as femininity no more

no more other gender

there's only supposed to be
one gender today
girls are turnin into guys
guys are turnin into girls
guys wearin earrings and dresses
they get sex-change operations
(you see them on oprah
and donahue)
not only on t.v.
you see girls walkin down the block
m.f.'n everybody

punchin and kickin
dirty mouthin ugly words i can't even pronounce
girls wanna go in the army and fight
they wanna be auto mechanics
and construction workers
  and truck drivers
    you got girls on the cover of muscle magazines
              liftin weights
                  tryin to look like charles atlas
              **i can't take all that
              i like to know what
              gender i'm lookin at**
                  that's why i stay at home
                  all the time
                  and look at my wall

in addition to my collection of coca-cola girls
i also got gina (lollobrigida)
doris day and jean harlow
judy garland
(one when she was young
like in the wizard of oz
and one right before she died)
debbie reynolds
connie stevens
(she was always a pretty girl)
sophia loren

donna just sent me a beautiful coca-cola calendar
just like the old ones
she gets me all them calendars
the betty boop calendars
the marilyn monroe calendars

i like the way things were meant to be

**two genders
not one
two!**

when i lay down on my couch
  and set my eyes up at that wall
    i know that i'm a guy
      and all of them are girls
        and that makes me happy

wheels

me
i use my two feet to get around
that or other people drive me places
oh i used to have my own cars
are you kiddin?
i had plenty of cars
i knew how to take em apart
and put em back together again too
i still do
not these new toys they sell today
the old ones
american cars
that's what i drove
i had a 1944 ford i bought off a rich lady in manhattan
that car was a hundred percent solid steel
when she gave me her insurance papers
i couldn't believe it
cause in them days most people didn't have insurance
she had that thing insured for hail
earthquake and flood
that's how rich that lady was
i ran it into the ground!

another piece of solid steel i had was a used 1934 dodge
i cried over that car
  i cried
i felt like a king

drivin around in that rock
six tires (four on the ground
  one on the fender and one on the back)
    you couldn't pick them tires up
      they weighed over a hundred pounds!
        soon as the war started
          i couldn't afford to keep it no more

after some guy from new jersey
gave me the money for it and drove away
i cried

my favorite car of all times though
was my baby the 1955 buick riviera
it saved my life that car
new year's eve 1956
if that car wasn't built like a truck
you probably wouldn't be talkin to me right now

it was late at night
i was comin around the bend of an exit off the l.i.e.
and all of a sudden
bam
shibang
crunch
bam
shibang
crunch
there was construction goin on there
but i had no way of knowin
there were no lights
there were no bright signs
nothin!

what actually happened
my car mounted these twelve by twelves
and i just kept bouncin on this stuff
bam   bam
shibang shibang
crunch   crunch like that

my back seat popped out and cracked my head
i must've just blacked out
cause bein it was new year's eve and all
i guess i had a few drinks in me
did i mention that?
i was just layin there unconscious
on the exit ramp of the highway
in the front seat of my riviera
and before you know it this cop's pokin me with his stick
come on
come on
i'm sayin
naahhhh
i dun waaannna
i can't leave my caaaarrrrrr
i can't leave

wheels

my car was way up in the air
on top of the twelve by twelves
the wheels were off the ground
the door was dented in
the fender was bent outta shape
the back seat was practically in my lap
there was blood drippin down my face

so i grab the steering wheel
like i'm gonna drive myself outta that mess
the cop must've looked at me like i was outta my mind
there were two cops actually
one cop was nice
the other was nasty
so the nasty one **bops** me over the head
with his nightstick
so i say

**no no please officer
i didn't see any sign
there were no lights
i was gettin off the exit
cause i just left my brother's house
in new hyde park
he's a policeman!
he's a policeman!**

so the nice cop says

oh yeah

he takes my license
and they drive me all the way over to tony's house
in new hyde park
and knock on the door
rap rap rap
lucky for me the new hyde park cops
and the new hyde park firemen were havin their annual
new hyde park new year's party
right there in my brother's house
the nasty cop says

**i got somebody in the car here
says he's yer brother**

tony comes outside and says
**yeah yeah yeah
that's my brother**

so they turned me over to him
and then my brother and one of the firemen from the party
throw me into the back seat of a car
and drive me to long island jewish hospital

the doctor sews eighteen stitches into my scalp
and lets me go
(if my brother wasn't a cop i would've lost my license)

the next day
when we went to retrieve my car
it was gone
kaput — stolen!
the scavengers took my beautiful 1955 riviera
that was the first riviera ever made
and the best car i ever had
she was a beauty that piece of stone

(you know they say when a greek dies
they don't go look at the body
they all go and rob the furniture in the house)
you see all these cars ridin around
with bunches of guys inside
goin down the expressway lookin for abandoned cars
that's what they did to my riviera
they took my car right off that pile of twelve by twelves
that thing is a collector's item
the black shiny fins and pinstripes and whitewall tires
it even had power steering and a radio
gone
   disappeared
      wiped out!

no insurance
nothin!
in them days you didn't have to have insurance
till you had your first accident
(only today the faggots make it mandatory)
if you bumped a guy's fender or somethin
you gave him a coupla bucks
and that was that

i don't bother with cars no more
if i wanna go anywhere i take the subway
otherwise people come and pick me up
the cars they make today
 are plastic junkyards on wheels
   that's what they are
      nothin can compare to that riviera
         nothin!

like a pit bull

i used to be like a pit bull

kill em

kill em

kill em

you know — fierce

but then i made a vow

not to get like that no more

cause i was bad

i was really bad

one time i nearly killed a guy!

i was goin out with this girl

i was just startin out with girls back then

i thought i had to be the big protector and everything

there was a standing order in them days

every guy had his own girl

and nobody should mooch in

so one day

i walked over to pick her up

and i caught this guy right there in her backyard

talkin to her and everything

so i jumped him

i got him down on the ground

i set him on his back with my legs to either side

and i started punchin his face in

punchin

punchin

punchin

i just kept punchin away at his face

i was totally mad

i was wigged outta my mind

i just kept punchin

punchin

punchin

till some neighbors came and pulled me off him
the guy was weepin and moanin
there was blood all over the place
i really think if they hadn't pulled me off
i would've killed him
(of course i had a gallon of guinea red in me at the time
i'm sure that didn't help)

the next day i saw him
and his front teeth were missin
his nose was broke
he had this big bump on his head
a shiner on each eye
and you know what?

he wanted to be my friend!

i made a big impression on him i guess
what are you gonna do?

that's when i made up my mind
not to get like that no more
i been in alotta fights in my day
if i got my hands around your neck (for some reason)
i'd never let go
unless you cut my wrists off
i fought like a caged animal
but that was the closest i ever came to killin somebody
when i got into a fight
all my mind could see was hate
nothin else but hate

hate hate hate hate

everything else disappeared

so i made up my mind

no
more
violence

a few months later my temper swelled
and i got put to the test
i was partners with this guy in an auto repair shop
up on northern boulevard
i bought the station originally on my own

like a pit bull

a few years earlier just as a gas station
but then my girlfriend introduced me
to this guy who was a friend of her family
a real drifter this kid
a big strong hillbilly from maryland
but he was a good mechanic!
he seemed like a hard worker to me
so i got in with him
and within a few weeks we went partners
we became drinkin buddies too

just as soon as i teamed up with that guy
the place started fillin up with cars
he kept takin in orders for motor jobs
muffler jobs
carburetors
all different repairs
takin money off people (deposits and all)
i figured
jeez this is great!
but then a few days into bein partners
i come into work and he's not there
i call him up
nobody answers!
turns out
he skipped town!

i got two garages
and a parking lot fulla cars
and he skipped town
with all the friggin money

now it's two years after that — right?
and i ain't seen hide nor hair of this friggin guy
i'm across the street in joey's bar
and guess who comes walkin in
wearin a smile as wide as georgia?

i took him outside
put him up against the brick wall
grabbed him by the throat
and started goin at him with my bare hands
punchin
and punchin
and punchin
blood's pourin down his face
two years of bein pissed off at this guy
spilled right outta me onto his face

and then somethin hit me
i heard somethin like . . .
a little voice inside of me
and it was sayin . . .

      you better not

      you better not do it man

      get a hold of yourself

      stop!

      stop it!

so i dropped my hands
i looked around and i said to him
    now you wanna hit me?
    here take a shot

he looked at me like i was crazy
    c'mon punch me
    take a shot!

i stood up against the wall
and let him take a swing at me
i took the full blow
then i said
    okay
    now are you happy?

  he said
      yeah

  i said
    okay
    let's go in
    and have a coupla beers

and that was the end of that

ever since that episode
no matter what people say or do to me
if they curse at me
 steal from me
  talk behind my back
    double-cross me
      whatever it is i don't lift a finger
        i never lifted another finger to anybody again

and that was over forty years ago!

ask not

don't forget
when he made that quote
everybody cheered
okay when a war breaks out and you're a guy
you hafta go to war
or the country'll be up shit creek
the masses cheer whenever the soldiers come home
so they cheered for him cause he was a big war hero
i can understand that
jumpin off of the p.t. boat and all of that
but then he got up on that pedestal to be president
and everybody cheered
so that's when he said

**ask not what your country
can do for you
ask what you can do
for your country**

remember that?
everybody cheered
but i said
**up your ass
you're the president
you do
you do you do
son of a bitch**
what the hell did he mean by that?
i never knew what he meant
to this day i don't understand its meaning
maybe you can help me understand
cause he never explained it
i mean what can a two-dollar bettor do for the country?
i been thinkin about this for over thirty years now

the  answer :

nothin!

what did he want me to do?
i'm slavin my ass off workin my whole life
every friggin job under the sun
and all he wants to know is what can i do for him
that son of a bitch
i already gave uncle sam a third of my salary my whole life
and for what?
for pumpin my father fulla mustard gas?
for takin tommy to vietnam and breakin his bones?
for sittin on jury duties my whole life?
i paid my dues
i gave to my country

he was the president!

he shoulda done somethin
he shoulda done somethin for me
and everybody else who pays taxes
but all he said was

we're going to the moon
the moon
the moon

that's all he cared about
the moon
the moon
the moon

the great stomach explosion of '64

the dallas cowboys did it to me
christmas eve 1964
my whole family's in the kitchen
eatin spaghetti'n meatballs
i'm eatin my plate in the living room
cause i'm watchin the play-off game on the couch
(you know what a giants fan i am)
i call in to my sister nette
to bring me some more of that hot pepper
the dallas cowboys are doin a job on the giants
and it's killin me
i sprinkle alotta that hot pepper on my plate
my brother tony's across the street in the bar
playin santa claus for the kids
(in them days they had a dining room
in the back of the bar for people to throw parties)
i keep lookin out the window every few minutes
to see if tony's comin back home
i look at the game
i go back into the kitchen
scoop out some more meatballs with the hot pepper
i go back into the living room to watch the game
only to discover dallas picked up another seven points
i couldn't believe it!
i feel somethin turnin inside my stomach
the giants are at third and fifteen
and they're only at their own forty-yard line
they're dyin!

i'm screamin at the t.v. set
what're ya blind?
i could drive a truck
through that hole!
go for the bomb
go for the bomb
you asshole!

meanwhile
whatever's twistin inside my stomach is really goin at it
i feel like i'm gonna faint
i look outside the window
to see if my brother's on his way over
i'm thinkin
maybe i ate too much
cause i feel kinda bloated
i don't know what the hell is goin on
i walk into the kitchen
my mother turns around
looks at me and says
whatsa matta nicky?

i says
i don't know
i gotta go to the bathroom

i lean over the terlet cause i'm feelin nauseous
i put my fingers down my throat
just to get it over with
        all
          of
            a
              sudden
                 everything
                turns
                red
there's blood
all over the bathroom!
nette brings me a chair so i can sit
while i'm throwin my guts up
my brother finally comes home
he calls the police
(since he's a cop himself we got fast service)
my mother's tryin to force cognac down my throat

turns out
a gastric ulcer the size of a quarter
was growin right on top of a blood vessel
inside my stomach
and when the lesion finally ruptured
it made my whole insides blow apart

when the ambulance came
the medics wanted to give me oxygen
but i threw the mask away
so i could hear them tryin to figure out
what hospital to take me to

the great stomach explosion of '64

cause the blood banks were low
on account of the subways bein on strike
the city was all jammed up with cars
nobody could get anywhere
and to make matters worse
guess what nicky d.'s got?

the second-rarest blood type on the whole stinkin earth!
r.h.b. negative
it's great blood
(in terms of immunity it's top-shelf)
but it's almost impossible to find

i said
will ya quit squawkin
and just take me to elmhurst hospital
so they took me to the emergency ward
at east elmhurst hospital
that's when all the fun began
cause they didn't have any r.h.b. negative blood
they ask me

> *who else in your family is r.h.b. negative?*

there's only two people in my whole family who's got it
but cecilia's too small
and vinny's daughter was just a kid at the time
so my brother tony starts makin phone calls all over town
lookin for some r.h.b. negative blood
my union didn't have any
none of the other hospitals had any to spare
finally . . .
he locates some at the blood bank
at his precinct up in harlem
but since the subways are on strike
and the streets are all jammed up
they have to send a messenger to go fetch it

meanwhile they're shovin tubes in me
up in here

down into there   down my mouth

up my nose

then they put me on the pump to pump my stomach

bi-boom-shhoooo

       bi-boom-shhoooo

              bi-boom-shhoooo

first the blood comes out red

then it comes out amber

then it comes out white

that means you're down to normal stomach fluid

so you can stop it right there

then when the blood came in

they pumped that into me

then they brought me upstairs to this other place

where they tried to medicate me

with a whiskey glass of maalox

when i realized what i was drinkin i said

no no,
maalox
isn't good for me!

but it was too late

i went into another hemorrhage

bleedin all over again

they rush me back downstairs

they stick the tubes in me

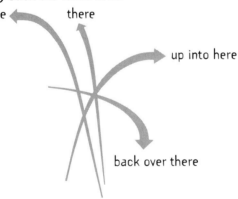

here   there

                      up into here

                   back over there

then they hook me up to the pump all over again

bi-boom-shhoooo

     bi-boom-shhoooo

          bi-boom-shhoooo

          red

               amber

                   white

pump in the new blood

disconnect me

bring me back upstairs

and force more maalox

and all kinds of garbage down my throat

the great stomach explosion of '64

for a coupla days i seemed to be doin okay
but i could tell somethin was terribly wrong
they didn't know what i had
there were two doctors on my case
one guy really wanted to be a jockey at the racetrack
the other was from south africa
(dr. mzracki — he was better than the other guy)
i tell him
doctor
don't let me outta this hospital
the way i am
you gotta cut me up
and see what i got in there
the maalox and all this shit you're givin me
might stop the hemorrhaging
for a little while
but that's only short-term measures
i can tell it's gonna burst again
please doc
i don't wanna go home till you cut out
whatever i got inside of me
please!
please!

dr. mzracki says

> **try to get some sleep mr. detommaso**
> **we're still running some tests**
> **through the lab**
> **and then we'll see what the story is**
> **okay?**

later that night i call for the nurse
she comes in
and says

> *whatsa matta?*

i say
> **i feel like i'm gonna . . .**
> **like i'm gonna . . .**

she pats me on the head
and says

> *c'mon now*
> *everything's gonna be alright*
> *try to get some sleep*

as soon as she leaves i feel it comin on again
i press the beeper by the side of the bed

no nurse . . .
i keep pressin it . . .

beep **beep** **beep** **beep** **beep**

finally the nurse comes in with a look on her face like
now what?

they treat you like a little kid when you get sick
ever notice that?
    i say
       please
       you gotta listen to me
   she says
        let me give you some more . . .
    i say
       please!

i grab the little bedpan by the side of the bed and say
      just wait a minute nurse

i put the pan down on the bed
      now wait a minute nurse
      now watch this!

i put my finger down my throat and

      everything turns red
      there's blood all over the place
      it doesn't stop comin

the nurse starts screamin

get the doctor!
get the doctor!

they wheel my whole bed into intensive care
and plug me full of tubes all over again
bi-boom-shhoooo
   bi-boom-shhoooo
      bi-boom-shhoooo
        red . . . amber . . . white

the great stomach explosion of '64

i turn to dr. mzracki and say
now you know what i'm tellin ya doctor
he says

    you're right
    you're right
    tomorrow we're going to do the job on you
    we're going to cut it out

later that night i hemorrhage again
worse than all the other times
i'm like a bloody niagara falls
i'm screamin and moanin
they rush me downstairs
they come at me with the tubes
they hook me up to the pump (the whole rigmarole)
only this time i black out
i'm not unconscious (i'm not in a coma)
it's more like trauma
which isn't good for the doctors
cause they wanna hear you scream
they want you to say ouch so they can tell what's goin on
cause you know with a stomach ulcer problem
they don't even anesthetize you
they don't give you no drugs (unless they're gonna operate)
they say if you're on medication it might make you
so tranquil you could hemorrhage in there
and nobody would know it

now as far as they can tell i'm out cold
  they're sayin i'm in shock
    but whatever you wanna call it
      at that moment . . .

i float up outta my body.

all the way up near the ceiling

above the lights
into a kind of hazy place
like underwater blurry
a place where there's
absolutely no pain whatsoever

i
look
down
and
i
see
myself
layin
there
with all the blood and all the tubes
and all the monitors and doctors
and nurses around me
i see the whole thing
i hear every word plain as day
i hear the doctor say to the nurse
what's the pulse?

the nurse is checkin me out (she can't believe it)
she does a double take
she checks me out again
she says
there's hardly any pulse

now you'd think i'd be scared right?
but i'm not
there's nothin that i fear
nothin!

the great stomach explosion of '64

i'm just watchin all this like it's some kind of movie
the doctor says

what's the pulse now?

the nurse says

there is no pulse

what about blood pressure?

there isn't any

you know from my seat in the balcony
i didn't give a shit which way the movie ended
it never occurred to me that i was practically dead
and if i was i wouldn't have cared

one of the nurses says

we're running real low
on the r.h.b. negative blood

dr. mzracki says

we have to get new blood in him fast
goddamn it
call for more emergency blood
immediately!
☞ **do this**
do that ☞ **get this**
☞ **get that**

when a messenger finally shows up with new frozen blood
the doctor says

we have to put this in him the way it is
we don't have a choice
(the blood didn't have a chance to thaw)
as soon as they start pumpin that cold blood into me
i can see myself shakin

i'm **boun** cin **up** and **down** on **the** bed

i see myself turnin blue
and then darker blue
and then purple

birrr **rup** birrr **rup** birrr **rup** birrr **rup**

they put that freezin cold blood into me
with no anesthesia
or nothin

suddenly everything just gets

real nice
and serene-like
i get a feeling of almost
an almost perfect feeling
like everything's just
the way it should be
peaceful
there's no pain
no fear
no troubles

i'm lookin down at myself
i'm lookin down at the nurses
and dr. mzracki

i'm hoverin sorta
right on top of the light
in suspended animation
like a chopper

you know how helicopters hover in one spot
like a hummingbird
well
i'm lookin down
and i see they're doin all kinds of things to me
but i can't feel a damn thing

the nurse says
> *i think i'm getting a pulse*
> *he's coming back . . .*
> *he's coming back . . .*

the great stomach explosion of '64

the next thing i know
i'm back in the recovery room in excruciating pain
thinkin
a second ago
i was floatin up on the ceiling
i didn't give a damn about anything
i didn't feel a thing
now i'm layin in this room
cryin and moanin like a sick old dog

dr. mzracki comes in

**you know we almost lost you there
but you pulled through**

they thought i was gonna die
but they were fulla shit
cause wherever i was
i came back
so i could live through some more agony
i guess

the next day they took out three-quarters of my stomach
and i survived!
i survived the operation of a thousand cuts
they did a perfect job on me
(only thing they did wrong
when they sutured me back up
they didn't stitch me all the way closed
that's why after thirty years
i'm still pullin sutures outta my stomach
i pulled out four or five just the other day
you should see the collection of sutures i got now
everybody laughs at me
i think i finally got to a big knot
i'm afraid if i pull it all the way out
it's just gonna make the hole even bigger)

after the operation i was still all wired up
not just up my nose
but in my stomach
my arms
it was a living hell!
i was in agonizing pain
my brother tony couldn't stand seein me like that
so he paid a private nurse to sit by my bed
read me magazines
and give me extra shots of painkiller at night
i was so frigged-up by that time
i took whatever they gave me

no questions asked
i remember one night
that nurse gave me a shot of some kind of narcotic
and i started gettin sorta floaty

i Floated outta my body again

only this time it didn't feel right
it wasn't natural
the drug was makin me leave my body
i could tell cause it wasn't peaceful
it was scary
i was sayin all kinds of things i didn't mean
i was strugglin with the private nurse
she had to hold me down
she slapped my face
she asked me later

> *you know what you were doin?*

i said
no no wha . . . what i do?

she said

> *you really don't know?*
> *you tried to pull out the tube*
> *and the intravenous*
> *you could've killed yourself!*

that was the closest i come to bein on drugs
is that how you are when you're on drugs?
you get all delirious
and you don't know what's goin on?
is that what drugs do?
they blank out your mind?
cause when i came to i didn't remember nothin
nothin!

when tony came to visit me the next day
i said
what the hell did you tell em to give me?

he says

> **i just wanted em to keep you from havin**
> **so much pain at night**
> **that's all**

i says
now you can pay em
to stay the fuck away from me
i'd rather have the pain

the next day when my family came to visit
they caught me

boun cin **up** and **down** on **the** bed

readin the newspaper
cause my horse won me fifty bucks
i was so excited

they looked at me like i was a ghost
the whole family seemed down in the dumps
like they was depressed i come out alive or somethin
i couldn't understand it
until the next day
(seventy-two hours after the operation)
my brother tony comes in with the whole gang
and a bottle of champagne

turns out
the doctor took a biopsy of the putrefied tissue
to see if any of it was cancerous
nobody told me
that on top of everything else
they were worried i might have cancer
so that morning when the tests came back negative
they all came to tell me the good news
then we had a big party right there in my hospital room

a coupla months later i was as good as new
the only drawback that came out of it was
i couldn't eat strong spices no more
other than that i was like a newborn baby
i came back from the dead
they fixed me up
gave me a new stomach and everything

i was thankful for all that
i was glad to be alive
but at the same time
in a way . . .
i didn't give a damn
i still don't give a damn
if i get run over by a truck tomorrow
i'm just not scared of dyin like i used to be
i like livin
but
i just don't need to hang on to
this piece of dirt called earth forever and ever
that's all . . .

when my time comes
i won't fight it
i'll just let go
 float up high (like a chopper)
   look down at this here ant farm
     one last time and say
        sigh o nara man
         sigh o nara

don't ever say i was an alcoholic

i was just a weekend horseshit artist
i didn't drink that much
until after they took out my stomach
cause the doctor said

> **you're as good as new**
> **we cut out all the dirt**
> **(the bad part of your stomach)**
> **sewed it all up so what you have left**
> **is as good as new**
> **like a baby's stomach**

the doctor never should've told me that
cause he made a monster outta me
when i came home from the hospital
i'd finish off a whole six-pack in one night

burlurp
burlurp
burlurp
burlurp

without stoppin

the doctor was right about one thing
i never had a bellyache
or no more problems with my stomach
but i was drinkin more and more
i was goin through a crisis
after almost dyin in the hospital
when i came home i didn't know what to eat no more
so i didn't eat
i was livin with my mother
but she wasn't feelin too good neither
so what was i supposed to do?
huh?

i didn't have a wife no more
i didn't have a stomach no more
all i had was the bar right across the street starin at me
twenty-four hours a day
i'd wake up in the morning
and that bar'd be starin right at me

so i'd hang out in the bar a lot
have four five beers

the guys'd go out in their cars to get chinese food
i'd stay in the bar and keep drinkin beer
then when i got all filled up i'd go in the terlet
throw it up
come back again and have **more beers**
more beers
more beers

my mother'd be out the window hollerin

nicky
c'mon home and eat!

i never came home
i'd sit in the bar all night **drinkin beer**
throwin up
drinkin beer
throwin up
drinkin beer
throwin up

it got so bad
i'd go across the street to the bar before i went to work
no breakfast
just a drink or two

as time went by i'd have a couple more drinks
a couple more
i'd look at the clock
put a nickel or dime in the phone and call in sick
stay in the bar all friggin day

so eventually **The New York Times**
started gettin wise to me
they were sayin
why don't you go to our place up in
connecticut for a little while?
they got their own dry-out place in connecticut
where they send their employees
they also got their own a.a. meetings
up on the eleventh floor
they wanted me to go to those too
i said
nah i don't need that
but i was curious
so i went up to the eleventh floor just to check it out
the president of the club asked me a few questions

don't ever say i was an alcoholic

i answered his questions the best i could
cause i got nothin to hide
you know me
i'm an open book!
the guy says

> *nick . . .*
> *to tell you the truth*
> *you're not an alcoholic*
> *but you might be borderline*
> *if you'd like you can sit in*
> *on one of our sessions*

so i said
alright let me try it

ooooohh man
never go to an a.a. session
it's enough to drive you to drink
i sat in on three or four of them meetings
f'get about it
for a normal person to sit in on one of them things
they're all alcoholics!

they all stand up there one at a time and say
my name is nicholas detommaso
i'm an alcoholic
they make you say that
and then they make you talk about your experiences
sssshhhhhhhhoooo
i'm up there talkin about drinkin six-packs on the weekend
that's baby stuff compared to the stories
these people had to tell!
one girl said she carried around a little bottle in her purse
used to bring it to work and keep it inside her desk
and every once in a while she'd open the desk
burlurp
burlurp
burlurp

one guy got up and said he was drinkin so heavy
one night in a bar someplace around times square
bombed out of his mind
the next thing he knew
a cop was hittin his shoes with a nightstick
and guess where he was?
guess?

he was sleepin on the grass in a park
somewhere in washington d.c.
he walked right outta times square

and boarded a plane to fuckin washington d.c.
without even knowin it
that's what blackouts do to you!
no recall whatsoever

another guy was a merchant seaman
one time he was out to sea and he ran outta booze
on this ship that was haulin fifty-five gallon drums of
100% HIGH OCTANE
the ship got caught in a real bad storm
this guy starts goin berserk cause he's got nothin to drink
he's gettin the d.t.'s
so he goes and opens up one of the high octane drums
pours some into a bucket
walks back down into the galley
opens a can of orange juice
mixes that in with the high octane and drinks it all up
and you know what?

the fuck didn't die
these people don't die!
you and me probably would've died

there was a guy who said he was drinkin sterno!
that stuff'd rip the shit outta me

another guy lost his fortune
he lost his wife
he lost his home
his boats
his cars
his reputation
i wasn't like that
i always could've stopped if i really wanted to
i just drank beer (mostly)
but then when my mother died
i felt so bad
a coupla days after we buried her
after i drank up the last beer i had in the fridge
i called my brother vinny to bring over a six-pack
it was snowin so he just dropped off the beer
and zipped right back home

i drank that six-pack by myself
i looked up at the clock
it was just after midnight
i remember thinkin
i gotta go to work in the morning

don't ever say i was an alcoholic

i didn't eat no food
i had nothin but beer in me
now i'm gettin like ray milland
you know *lost weekend*
that movie when ray milland sees bats on the walls
and he's got bottles of whiskey in chandeliers
he's got bottles hidden all over
i'm lookin all over the apartment just like ray milland
only in my movie there isn't a drop left in the house
the bars are all closed
i get frantic and call one or two people
but nobody can come down to bring me a beer or nothin
so now i'm gettin even more frantic (fidgety-like)
i look under the bed
i look in all the cabinets
nothin!
till finally underneath the kitchen cupboard
i find a bottle of green d' mint

so i open
that bottle of green stuff
and drink it all down

the next morning i was too sick to go to work
my sister annemarie came over to take care of me
as soon as she sees me she calls my brother tony
she calls my brother vinny
they come over
tony says

**let's call the new york times
send him to the farm up in connecticut**

annie stuck up for me

*nah nah nah
is that how ya treat a brother?
i'll take care of him*

vinny wanted to call an ambulance
but annie wouldn't let him
she took care of me right there in the apartment

i got to thinkin about how my mother brought up six kids
all by herself in a small apartment like this
i thought about what it must've been like
havin my father die on her so young
i felt so bad cause my mother died before i ever
really got to do the things i wanted to do for her

i thought
if she's watchin me
what would she see?
she'd see her son
layin on the kitchen floor
drinkin green d' mint
gettin bombed outta his mind

i thought
how can i do this?
after that lady
devoted most of her life to me
i can't even go to work
this is no good
this is no good

so right then and there
i made a vow to straighten up
i vowed to never touch another drop of anything
and you know what?
i stopped drinkin cold turkey just like that

up on the eleventh floor
they couldn't believe i could stop just like that
jeez nick
how can you quit
just like that?
that's it
i made that vow
and i'm keepin it

that's when i found out there's food in the world
i started takin care of myself
i found out about all them nice things
bacon'n eggs
pancakes
all them nice things
sure you feel good while you're smashed
but after you wake up
you're still in the same old shit
so what's the use of kiddin yourself?

it's been over twenty years now
and i haven't had a drop of anything ever since
(other than ginger ale and pepsi)
not one drop
not one drop

on retirement

you're a painter
he's a shrink
i'm a longshoreman
the guy next door delivers
fish at four in the morning
everybody's got a job to do
but you can't just do your job

you gotta do it **good!**

if you wanna be a painter
you gotta be a <u>good</u> painter
you wanna be a harmonica player
you gotta be a <u>good</u> harmonica player
otherwise . . .
don't be that

you wanna be a bus driver
be a <u>good</u> bus driver
this is what i did on most all the jobs i had in my life
i took on everything!

- when i was a kid i shined shoes for a nickel

- i was an automobile mechanic

- i owned a gas station

- i worked on the docks for four years
  as a longshoreman with the mafia

- i worked for uncle sam in the post office

- i was a presser in a tailor shop

on retirement

- i did house painting (interiors and exteriors)

- i painted the 1939 world's fair (the pylon
  and the perisphere)

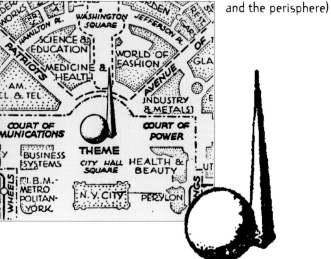

- i drove beer barrel trucks for pabst blue ribbon
  (it was the hoffmann brewery back then)

- i drove trucks and parked cars at radio city

- i chopped down trees for the c.c.c.

- i was a die setter for walde's zipper factory

- whatever i did
  i did it the best i could
  till i got disgusted with it
  and went on to do somethin else

- eventually i settled into one job
  i worked for **The New York Times**
  in receiving for thirty years
  until a steel door broke my neck
  and i got disgusted with the same routine
  sloggin back and forth to times square
  day after day in the snow and the rain

i got fed up!

and when you get fed up
that's when you can't do your job good no more
when you get fed up
you look in the mirror
you see some guy who ain't gettin any younger
and that's it
that's when you feel like quittin

but all you really know how to do is **work**

work

work

work

work

work

work

that's all you know how to do

every day you wake up in the morning

the alarm clock rings

you don't wanna go to work

but you gotta go — right?

so you keep workin cause you're scared

you go to work

but you're fed up

and then one day you just wake up and do it

you retire

after all them years of workin you finally retire

most people right after they retire

they wake up in the morning

they think their life is over

they think they made a big mistake by quittin

but if you don't jump off a bridge

you find out <u>that's</u> when all the fun begins!

i wake up in the morning and say

,wow
i'm still alive!

whatever i was restricted from doin

all them years i was workin

all them things i could never do

that's what i do now

my brother vinny went berserk when he retired

he started goin cuckoo

he got sick

just the other day he says to me

he says

nicky

i think i made a big mistake

i don't know what to do with myself

i shoulda stayed on the job

i yelled at him

what d'ya mean?

on retirement

what d'ya mean
you don't know what to do?
you got your own home
you got a backyard
you could plant vegetables
you can grow things
you can bang nails in the wall
you can paint your house
you can make your own hours

vinny just shrugged his shoulders
and gave me some more things to fix
i barked at him
what the hell's the matter with you?
you should do what i did before i retired
i saved seven weeks vacation
that was due me
that way i didn't hafta go back
and say good-bye to the sons a bitches
and when that first mondee came
the alarm clock rang early in the morning
like it did every morning
for the last thirty years
i took a shower
i got dressed just like i always did
ran down to the friggin subway in the snow
took a token outta my pocket
held it over the turnstile
for a coupla seconds
then i put it back in my pocket
and ran all the way home
like a nine-year-old
scrambled two soft eggs
with four strips of bacon
made pancakes
put my feet up on the table
watched a movie
and had the time of my life
that's what i told vinny he should do

i remember all them years of aggravation
goin down the cold subways waitin for a train
that sometimes never came or was so overcrowded
i'd freeze my ass off waitin for the next one

sometimes i had to let **ten trains pass**
till there was one i could squeeze into
by the time i got to work
it was a miracle i didn't have the flu
so just for spite
i did the same thing every day that first week of retirement
i got dressed
went down to the subway
held the token over the turnstile
put it back in my pocket and ran home
mondee
        tuesdee
              wensdee
                    thursdee
                         and then on fridee
i went to times square with a box of subway tokens
threw the whole box in the middle of times square
and watched all the people scramble on the ground
like a pack of vultures fightin after crumbs
i kept one token for myself
put it in the turnstile
took the number **7** train one stop to vernon jackson
walked up the stairs
then sang **god bless america** all the way home

after years of back'n forth back'n forth
i could finally wake up in the morning without that feeling
of a knot in the middle of my stomach
i told vinny (like i'm tellin you now)
as of that day i was a free man
i'm free like a jaguar
like a cheetah in the jungle
and i been that way ever since

a coupla times (after i retired)
i got up early and called
The Times receiving department

hello mr. scuotto
this is detommaso
put me down sick today
ha he haaa HAA haaa he HA
he ooh he HAHA he
ooh ha ah

i'd hang up the phone laughin
it was such a good feeling to know that
i didn't hafta go there no more
i don't hafta do nothin i don't wanna do

on retirement

that's what retire means
retire means nothin

> ## retire = nothin

today
when that alarm clock rings in the morning
i look at the clock
then i shut it off
and say **the hell with it**
i don't <u>hafta</u> go to work no more
i got no time clock
i can eat when i want
go to sleep when i want
wake up when i want
watch t.v. when i want
walk around when i want
cook up some meatballs'n ziti when i want
talk to the girls when i want
go into town when i want
work on fixin up a broken piece of junk when i want
put barbra streisand on the turntable when i want
go to offtrack betting when i want
go out to long island when i want
read the paper when i want
i can do anything i want
whenever i want
i'm retired and
i'm single!

ye old picture album

<u>mom and pop</u>
that's my mom and pop
(jessie and freddie)
when they got married

all my brothers and sisters look like my father
even my sister nette looks like my father
i'm the only one who took after my mother
look at those eyes
those are my eyes!

they used to put you in front of a canvas
in a studio in them days
before they took your picture they talked to you
they waited till just the right moment
not like today
today it's snap — you're in
flash — you're out

<u>grandpa</u>
there's my grandfather nicky
that's who they named me after
that guy
see that stone
that's a stone man
he was a tough son of a bitch
he used to wash his face in the rain water
that landed in a fifty-five gallon tank
out in his backyard
(next to the peach trees)
the tank was wooden
but he was made of stone

pop
there's my father
freddie detommaso
i'm the only one in the family
who never knew my father
i only remember him visiting me one time
in the hospital
he took me for a walk
i remember holdin his big hand
then in 1931
while i was still a little scrawny kid
layin in pain
flat on my back
in the pediatric ward of the hospital
my mother came and told me

nicholas . . .
your father passed away

he was only thirty-three years old
if it wasn't for these pictures
i wouldn't even know what he looked like
all i know is what i was told
and things i dug up on my own

he was a master mixer just like his father
you see that building
that's on vernon avenue
that's the paragon paints building
my father and my grandfather
ruled that whole building
they were the top master mixers for years
they were high-tech people
but between mixin all them paints
drinkin all his homemade brew he used to make
and takin in all that mustard gas in world war I
my father's lungs were all fucked-up
that's why he died so young

about fifteen years ago
i decided to go down to the board of health
and get a copy of his death certificate
under cause of death it said
he died of a lung abscess

then in small print right underneath contributory factors
it said

complications due to
mustard gas inhalation
in world war I

nobody would've known why he really died
if it wasn't for me snoopin around
playin sherlock holmes

you wanna laugh how contradictory things are?
i dug up a copy of my father's honorable discharge
and under vocation it said
he was a painter
they got that right
but under physical condition when discharged
it said   received no wounds

**what a crock of shit that was
he was all gassed up**

other than how he died
i can't tell you nothin else about my father
firsthand

i'm the keeper of the family documents
especially birth and death
i got papers from all the different burials
it cost $2,237.71 to bury my mother in 1970
when carmella passed away
it only cost $653.83
that was in 1950
when my father passed away
i think in them days it just cost 32¢ to bury him!
oh here it is — $68.87
you see how the cost of dyin
has gone outta control?

these are from the guest book when my father died
november 17th 1931
we didn't use no funeral parlors in them days
the body was just laid out in the house
so when people came into the house
to show their last respects
they gave money to help pay for the burial
this is what they were givin
$10 $2.50 $5 $3
lookit these names
all italian
Rizzo
Pagnari
Rosso
Natalizzio
Barro

all our different names
here's my father's naturalization papers
when he came from italy
this is what they gave him at ellis island back then
the united states of america certificate of naturalization
spelled his name

THOMASO

that's wrong the way they typed it out
in the army they spelled it

Tomaso

that's wrong too
everything was all screwed up with our name
look at what it says here
in the queens vocational yearbook

Thomas Joseph Clav..
Thomas Alfred Confor..
Thomas Francis Cronin
Vincent Peter Digilio
Anthony Angelo Delli Gatti
Thomas Dominic DeQuatro
Nicholas John DeThomas
Michael Patrick Dwyer
Alfred Anthony Fulgentiz
Salvatore Louis Garramone
Robert Joseph Gibbons
John Thomas Hyland
Francis Patrick Irving
... Henry Ke...

that's how the catholic nuns spelled my name
when i went to saint mary's school
they wanted to make me irish like them
look what they did
every friggin report card it says

Nicholas John DeThomas
(First name)   (Middle name)   (Last name)

they did that to all my brothers and sisters
it's not until we got into the business world
that anybody required proper i.d.
after we all got outta school
we went downtown to get our birth certificates
and found out our name was really

DETOMMASO

all this time growin up we thought we were

DeThomas

my brother vinny had it spelled

DiTommaso

everybody was different
even now sal uses one m
nette still keeps

DeThomas

ye old picture album

**we're all screwed up in this family
the gravestones will never match
nobody will know we're all one family**

midwife
this is the midwife that delivered me and tony
i think she delivered all of us
there were no hospitals in them days
they used to have the babies right in the house
today they want thousands of dollars
to have a baby in a hospital
what are they kiddin?
they used to do it in caves
on mountaintops
you don't need all this hardware
and dough ray me to be born right

not my brother but my uncle tony
when my aunt lillie married tony
that was bad news
cause tony was a serious gangster
in new jersey he was known for
bein a real tough motherfucker
he ruled newark
only thing that kept him in check around here was
he was afraid of new yorkers
thank god
on the other side of the river
he did whatever came to his mind
after he tried to break into new york he mellowed down
this city can do that to a guy like him

all gone
look at that
that's 1917
that's my mother
at fourteen or fifteen
there's her sister katerina
these are all jersey people
they're all gone now
gone
off the face of the earth

harp
i used to play the harmonica
professional!
i played with a guy on guitar
and a drummer
no readin music or anything fancy
i played by ear
and it came outta my mouth

the great occupational divide
after the war
me and my brothers tony
vinny and sal
all got jobs workin for the post office
then we all split up
and went to different jobs
tony went to the police
vinny went to the racetracks
sal went to mixin inks as a master mixer
like my father
and i went off to do a million different things

pit bull
see this pit bull
he was strong as a gorilla
and calm as a lollipop
he used to sleep with me
he was a pure pit bull
you know
them dogs are no more ferocious than a ball of cotton
it's not the pit bull that's the killer
it's people
these friggin people today get the dogs all hyped-up
they give em crack
and taunt em with pounds of raw meat
they train em to kill
i know pit bulls
if it wasn't for people
they'd be a hundred percent angel

ye old picture album

vinny at war
here's a picture of my brother vinny in germany
screwin around with a mine detector
lookin for mines

> tony at war
> here's tony with some of his buddies
> on the heavy cruiser

vinny just after the war
there's vinny in germany wearin a german helmet
(after they beat the germans
they took their helmets and belts home as souvenirs)

> me
> don't i look like a tough asshole?
> ## mr. tough guy
> they used to give me plaid shirts
> to make me look not so tough
> i had a closet fulla them plaid shirts

angelo and his wife
this is a picture of angelo at his wedding
we used to call him **chink** cause of his eyes
he's still got them slanty eyes
only now he's a big husky tank
he's got a hundred different ailments
he's gotta take thirty different medications a day
his heart
his blood pressure
everything is messed up with him
and his wife's all crippled up with arthritis
ever since she was a little girl she's had that
i don't know why
she's so pretty
i cry whenever i see her
i help her down the steps when she goes to the doctor
she can hardly walk
the two of them've been through hell
all these years and all that hell
but they're still together
i like that about them two

> sal's kid
> here's my brother sal's kid
> with joe namath
> he was in joe namath's camp
> that's why they got that picture
> that's why he went to that camp
> to get this picture

black knights

here i am walkin over hunter's point bridge
with my black knights jacket
must've walked that bridge a thousand times
the bar across the street was our headquarters
whenever a meeting was called
the bartender had to keep rushin us pitchers of beer
one after the other
there was a piano in there
we sang songs
that guy next to me is one of the pollacks from greenpoint
after we'd punch the shit outta them
we'd shake hands and become buddies
play shuffleboard
sing songs
next day we'd go out and beat each other up again

coney island

this picture is from when i used to go to coney island
i went with my motorcycle and my friend buddy
it's good to see him with two arms
(a coupla years after this picture
his right arm got blown off by a grenade in the war)
see all these prizes i won
i was an ace pitcher
i knocked down everything they had on the board
they had to give me all the prizes
popeye and betty boop
finally the guy told us

**take a walk fellas
i don't wanna see ya
round coney island no more
or nobody'll have any more prizes
to give away**

ye old picture album

tough subject
here's a sketch that jimmy wilson tried to make of me
back in 1962
he could never finish me
you're the hardest subject i ever met in my life
that's what he said to me
he drew everybody's picture that worked at **The Times**

jimmy started out in 1955 as an elevator operator
(alotta black guys got jobs runnin elevators back then)
but after the elevators went electronic
he got a job drivin the jitney
he drove them friggin jitneys all over town
and on the side he would sketch people
he was talented
he got everybody's likeness
but he could never get me right
he got my profile good
but he never finished it
he was just here a coupla weeks ago with his wife
he kept sayin
nicky you were the toughest subject i ever had

maybe one day
he'll be able to finish me off right

all my nieces and nephews draw pictures for me
terry did this for me
tony's daughter lorraine did this for me in 1974
that's supposed to be a monster
she just got married
chrissy drew this horse
she always liked drawin horses
they all had talent with art
this was done by eddie in 1961
now he's a cop
he's got three girls of his own

now i'm the keeper of all the sonograms
this is a sonogram of the new baby
(terry) before she was born
when she was still in donna's stomach
ain't she somethin?

proof
i put this in here just to prove
that there is a nicky d. from l.i.c.
just like the post office delivers mail
that just says santa claus the north pole
the post office knows me too
look . . .

nicky d. from l.i.c.
that's all it says on this letter
and it got to me
that means it's official

change
this is a picture of my wife when we were young
took it on the roof of a building down on jackson avenue
where they built that fuckin skyscraper
that's how things change
you see the bridge
if you walked just over the bridge
my favorite pizza place used to be right there
then there was the rug store
that building over there used to be a dance hall
before they renovated it
and that building behind the parking lot
well it's still there today
but you know what it was years ago?
it was a convent for nuns — with a grotto
see all the flowers and everything
they had growin all around the place
see how it's changed
everything got destroyed
the nuns left town
saint mary's school is closed
 the diocese uses the building for offices now
   no more kids
      no more flowers
         no more singin hymns
            no more wife
               no more young

now and then

even with all the turmoil
with a depression
and then a world war
growin up in the hospital
no father
even with everything that i lived through
life was pleasant back then
there was none of this
what you have today
there was no crime (hardly)
no drugs
no a.i.d.s.
no crack dealers or baby molesters
you didn't need no car alarms
or double
triple
quadruple locks on your doors
there were no transsexuals
or televangelists or telemarketers
no toxic waste sites or nuclear arsenals
there was none of that
everything was true!

today
everybody's suspicious of everybody else
i don't give a shit if you're talkin to the holy ghost
there's no such thing as trust no more

today

before you get married you sign a prenuptial agreement
and then a postnuptial and a nuptial-nuptial
whatever happened to

till death do us part

whatever happened to fearin the lord?
fearin your parents?
fearin your teacher?

years ago

you'd be scared shitless
if you came one minute late to school
you had to put out your hand
the nun whopped you with the big red stick
BING
   BING
      BING

today

kids go to school with guns and knives in their lunchboxes
they're all doped up
teachers gotta say their hail marys
before they go into the classroom just to come out alive

i'd never go into teaching today
even back then i wouldn't have been a teacher
or a welfare worker
i didn't wanna get messed up with the public
after i worked for the post office i made a vow
no more jobs with the public sector!
i had the whole hell's kitchen area all along the docks
eighth and ninth avenue
from forty-fifth street up to fifty-ninth
even then i had some scary moments
goin down those alleyways
cause there were gangs all over that area
that was where they filmed *west side story* you know

we used to have gangs in long island city too
it was the wops against the irish and the pollacks
but that was only fistfights back then
they were honest beatings
there was no knives or molotov cocktails
we didn't use no cans of mace or chain saws
or beebee guns or uzies
we didn't beat on girls or blow up cars
we didn't use chains or knuckle raps
or whips or razor blades

if you were gonna get involved in a fight
you hadta do it with your hands!
that was your only weapon
you'd knock a tooth out
get scratched up here and there
maybe a black eye
that was the big catastrophe
today
they'll come and blow you away

in them days people had respect for the law
respect for elders
respect for family
respect for womanhood
years ago you hadta beg a girl to kiss her
it was a big thing to kiss a girl
today
girls're gettin pregnant at thirteen
either they get an abortion or there's no father around
them days you'd have a shotgun wedding
otherwise the kid's a bastard
that was a big thing back then
to be a bastard
today
they look at you funny if you got a mother and a father
and if you do got that
both parents hafta go to work just to pay the bills
the cost of everything is so goddamn high
i can't believe the price of things

greedy bastard landlords are killin people
with the rents they charge today
they're always knockin on your door
they want their eight hundred dollars
a thousand or more
for hundred-year-old rat holes with no heat
they don't worship god almighty
they worship . . .

corporations don't talk hundreds or thousands
or even millions
they're talkin **billions!**
trillions! billions of trillions!

if you're workin for three
four dollars an hour in a sweatshop
how the hell can you pay these tuitions
unless you cheat or steal?
you see these punks on times square
with fistfuls of hundred-dollar bills
they steal your wallet
they steal your car
they don't know what it means to go to work

meanwhile the government only does for the rich
they did away with the c.c.c.
they did away with the w.p.a.
they did away with the o.p.a.
(the office of price administration)
you go on one corner
you buy a pack of butts for a buck forty
right across the street the same pack is a buck fifty-five
then you go over there
it's two bucks
people can't do nothin about it
with the o.p.a you had ceilings!
today
the roof is cavin in

look
i got my little setup here
i got my rent-controlled apartment
i'm not worried about myself
i worry about my nieces and nephews
that's what i worry about
if this is what they're growin up in today
what's it gonna be like in twenty years?
sometimes i wish i could scoop em up in my arms
and bring em back to the old days with me
 back to a place where it was safe
   and people were good
     and things were what they were meant to be
        that's what i wish i could do
             take em back
                  take em back with me

ghost of a chance

that's my mother's bed
nobody's slept in that bed
for twenty-five years

me?
i sleep on the couch in the living room with the t.v.

after my mother died
i got rid of all the other beds
i stuck with the couch
i stuck with the apartment
i stuck with my mother till her dyin day
i didn't care what people thought
(a grown man livin with his mother)

when i was in the hospital all them years
she was the only one who dragged her ass back'n forth
over the queensboro bridge to come and visit me
my mother was the only one!
that's why i was so close to her
that's why when all my brothers and sisters left
and went out and got married and had their own families
i had to stay and make sure
there was food on my mother's table
that was the least i could do
cause i was the thorn in her side
and i guess i felt i had to make up for that
i was the one who put her through all that grief
i was the one she had to rush over to after every operation
after every complication
i was the one who needed all the special attention
i was the one who'd come home at three in the morning
with blood on my face stinkin of beer
i was the one she had to lose sleep over
night after night
                    year after year

just before she died
on top of her heart condition and her diabetes
she caught hold of a bad flu
so i called for an ambulance
and i'll never forget
as they were takin her out of this apartment on a stretcher

travel

i never leave
i'll never leave my shangri-la
only sometimes
sometimes i go to flushing
or visit my friends at times square
or i go out to long island for a coupla days
but nobody's gonna shanghai me over to europe
or them dirty islands down there
i'm stayin right here!
i been here for nearly sixty years
same apartment
and i'm never bored!
every day i discover something new
every day is a new adventure

alotta people bug me
why don't you go on vacation
you're single!
that's what they say
especially married men tell me
you're single!
you can go to florida
have a good time
you can go all over the world

if i wanted to go to egypt or someplace i'd go!
but i don't wanna go nowhere!
that's what <u>they</u> wanna do
because they're married men
<u>they</u> wanna do that
but they can't!

people are the same all over the earth
why do you have to
spend a million dollars
to go get mugged
someplace where they
don't speak english?

a view from the stoop

on
life
death
health
money
and
god

the lights swirlin all around the block
people gawkin at her
she couldn't even hardly breathe
was she thinkin about herself?

no
no
not at all

her last words were

who's gonna take care of nicky?

i almost broke down right then and there

she went into the hospital that night
and died early the next morning
that was january 5th 1970

you couldn't get me to sleep in that bed
i haven't slept on a bed for twenty-five years
i got a big seven-foot couch
i can pop a tape into my v.c.r. any time of night
i got my bedtime for bonzo pillow
my wizard of oz pillow
it's very comfortable in the living room
i don't need a bed
i don't need the extra width
cause i never move when i sleep
i stay perfectly still
whatever way i drop out
that's the way i wake up
i could sleep like that on the hood of a cadillac
why the hell would i wanna go all the way
out into the bedroom there
when i could sleep right in the living room?
i mean that bed's still in perfect condition
i keep that bed just the way it was when my mother died
it's in perfect shape
there's nothin wrong with it
 i just happen to like sleepin on the couch
  in the living room
   it's a big couch with alotta room
    that's all
     i got nothin against that bed
      i love that bed

if you wanna go to florida for a vacation
and get a nice tan okay
but this one wants to go to bermuda
and screw around with the natives
this one wants to go to india and get malaria
this one wants to go to europe and look at the art
she goes to look at the mona lisa
and it's got a little tag there
says it's on loan to the museum in new york
it's on loan to
the metropolitan museum!
what are you gonna do?
this one wants to go to israel
so she can get blown up on a bus
on the way over to cry on some wall
or float in a dead sea
go fuck yourself
you went to switzerland
well good for you
you traveled all around
but you look the same to me as you did before
so what came of it?
what changed?
you went through all that grief
of gettin on airplanes and flyin and everything
you could've got killed!
and nothin came of it
cause the same sun that shines over there
shines right here
it shines on top of the swiss mountains
it shines in greenpoint
it shines on the beach in coney island
it shines on the moon

what are you talkin about?
i can sit on my stoop and get the same thing
why would i wanna go through all the trouble
of goin to airports and buyin tickets
and gettin suntan lotion
stuffin suitcases with rolls of toilet paper
and special plugs
why would i wanna bother gettin passports
passport photos and vaccinations and visas
writin up itineraries
or gettin all kinds of insurance
traveler's checks
why would i wanna spend my money on postcards
and camera cases and rolls and rolls of film
and foreign dictionaries

foreign maps
foreign this
foreign that
when i can walk around the corner
and pick up a gallon of virgin olive oil straight from italy
all the korean vegetables i can eat
a chinese eggroll
indian food
swiss chocolate
wiener schnitzels
you name it!

i don't hafta

go nowhere!

i got everything i need right here
why would i put myself through all that trouble
of doin this and doin that
when i get the same sun
that comes in through these two windows
  by sittin on my own couch
    in my own home
        drinkin my own cup of coffee
            smokin my favorite cigarette?

this building

i know this building
i've lived here since i was a kid in knickers
i know each wire
i know every fuse
every little crack in the wall
i can tell you where every leak on the friggin roof ever was
and will be
i know this building
i know its smelly hallways
its paper-thin walls
i know what spices are used in each apartment
i know when everybody leaves for work
and when they come back home
i know the family fights
and the drunken arguments
and the ambulances parked out front
i know where the property line begins and ends
back behind that overgrown jungle of a garden
i can tell you when this house was built
how many times it was bought and sold
for how much
and who the landlords were
i can tell you how many steps are on each floor
and when i last swept them
i can tell you when the mailmen changed
and what their names were
i can tell you when the boiler was replaced
and when the basement's gonna leak
and how many people can take a shower
until there's no more hot water left
i know this building
i've lived here practically all my life

RECEIPT

RENT R

we just wanted to have fun
how did i know what was gonna happen?
i could've had this whole building for three thousand dollars
the bar across the street for five thousand
but i wasn't real estate conscious

we were just havin fun!

we just wanted to play stickball and kick the can
we just wanted to put a bottle of beer
under the stoop and play johnny on the pony all night
that's all
we just wanted to have a little fun
who was thinkin about real estate?

this whole block

RENT RECEI

i could've bought
this whole block
for twenty grand!

but i just paid rent
i been payin rent for fifty years
and what do i have to show for it?

receipts!

that's what i got
nothin but a whole lotta receipts!

RENT RECEIPT

RENT RECEIPT

RENT REC

broadway plays

broadway plays
are hazardous

broadway
plays

* i never get myself involved with
more than six or seven people at once
if somethin's goin on with the population on the earth
i can read about it in the paper
that's enough for me
stay away from the throngs
that's what i say
(unless you're a red cross worker)

to your health!

what's the matter with you?
what do you think
i'm gonna waste my time watchin
a bunch of idiots runnin around a stage?
i don't go where there's crowds no more*
the air is bad enough
you sit in them friggin shows
inhalin the fumes
three four hundred dirty diseased
sick mother bastards sittin all around you
and you got the balls to holler at me
cause i smoke
get the hell outta here
i wouldn't go into one of them junk houses
if i had a helmet and a tank on my back
you're pickin up more cancer cells and a.i.d.s.
and all kinds of viruses
than if you sat at home and **ate**
four packs of cigarettes a day

a deal with god

god . . .

god . . .
i know you're there

pssst
god . . .

it's me
nicky d.
(the one from l.i.c.)

i'll make a deal with you god:

if you don't let me get no more ailments
or operations
or bein in hospitals
or things like that
you know cause well . . .
i mean
maybe you can pick on somebody else for a change
somebody that never had any of these diseases
and catastrophes

cause god . . .
if you don't mind me sayin so
i think i've had my share of them things all my life
god . . .
so i'll make a deal with you god:

you keep me alive and healthy
and i'm gonna use these two good hands you gave me
to help people
and i ain't gonna ask for no green
i'll accept lollipops and hershey bars
but other than that
there'll be no charge
i ain't gonna ask for no exchange of funds
i'm just gonna help people
and watch em smile
cause that's reward enough for me!

but god . . .

god . . .

the day
the day
the day i start
chargin people
for my services

that day
you can take the whole thing away from me
i'm all yours
whatever you want
my lungs
my heart
my liver

actually
just do me a favor
if that day should come god
you can just take the whole kit and caboodle
take the whole thing and call it a day

is it a deal god?

god?

god?
do we got ourselves a deal?
god?

well
i'll keep my end of it
and we'll call it a deal
okay god?

i'll keep up my end
i'll keep up my end of it

mr. fixit

people break things

who use things

to people

i got my training in electronics
i don't need manuals or books
if i can get inside something
i usually can fix it
otherwise it was a piece of garbage to begin with
that tape deck of yours was a piece of garbage
but i fixed it anyway
let me show you what to do if it happens again
just take off that black thing on top
and look for the prongs
open them up
then snap them back in
then you can put a little matchbook cover
or a little toothpick in there so it don't pop out
cause that's your only problem
the contacts in there were too spread open
that's all it was

they throw em out

and i fix em

and give em away

never buy anything that's
got things merged with it
like clock radios
console t.v. sets
washer dryer units
f'get about it
cause on them clock radios
when the radio goes
you're stuck with the clock
same with console t.v.'s
one thing interferes with the other
now they got these t.v. - c.d. - v.c.r. - microwave -
refrigerator - answering machine doodahs
the whole twentieth century in one machine
pick it up for christmas
good for the whole family
**who the fuck
do they think they're kidding?**

everything that lives dies

a cat in the neighborhood dies
so everybody starts to whisper and say things
    someone says

did it smoke?

  someone else says

yeah it smoked

so what's that mean
it died from smoking?

then this other cat dies
everybody starts to whisper
    someone says

did it smoke?

  another one says

*no
it didn't smoke
but it drank!*

oh i see
like that explains it

as soon as you die
everybody starts to whisper
till they figure out why you died
like . . .

if you just didn't smoke
or
*you didn't drink
maybe you wouldn't have died*
or
if you didn't eat cheeseburgers
or
you didn't live in new york city
***maybe then
you'd still be alive!***

but today
you can't just let the people enjoy themselves

no!

everywhere you go there's pressure
    don't eat this
    don't eat that
    don't smoke
    don't this don't that

i used to be able to buy a hundred cigarettes
for a quarter
buy a whole bag of tobacco
pour it into the rolling machine
KA TING
  KA TING
    KA TING
      KA TING
pull on the little rubber thing
DING
   DING
and the butts'd just come rollin out
one at a time
no friggin guilt trips from the surgeon general
you didn't have all these signs all over the place
in them days you did what you wanted to do
today there's

NO SMOKING

even in people's houses
i was over at my niece's place about a month ago
and after i made spaghetti'n meatballs
for the whole family
gina comes over to me and says

        uh . . .
        uncle nicky . . .
        uh . . .
        if you wanna smoke
        can you please go in the hall from now on?

i couldn't believe it!
i said
what the hell are you talkin about?
you want me to go out into the hallway
and sit on the steps
every time i wanna have a smoke
instead of sittin on the couch with my feet up
enjoyin myself with my family all around me
what the hell is goin on here?

she just looked at me and didn't say nothin
so i said
okay okay
i'll do you a favor
i'll go in the hall
and smoke my cigarette
like i'm some kind of a criminal!

she's still not sayin nothin

everything that lives dies

so i say
gina
let me ask you somethin
when you go to work tomorrow
and you throw your token in the subway
and you get off at times square
and walk up to your office
you mean to tell me you hold your breath
the entire four blocks from the subway
or are you chokin from the
carbon monoxide and diesel fuel and lead
comin out the back of them
ugly dirty filthy buses?

two weeks later i'm out at gina's place again
puttin up shelves
she comes over to me
and this time she says

> *uh . . .*
> *uncle nicky*
> *uh . . .*
> *if you hafta smoke*
> *can you smoke outside from now on?*

so now when i'm with my family
i gotta go out into the garage
into the zero degree temperature
and freeze my butt off
just to smoke a cigarette

today
every pack of cigarettes the surgeon general says

> SMOKIN CAUSES CANCER OF THE LUNG, HEART DISEASE,
> EMPHYSEMA AND INTERFERES WITH PREGNANCY

what the surgeon general forgot to say was

> ALL OF US WALKIN ON THIS EARTH HAVE CANCER

if i took you right now to a coroner
and he split you down the middle
and checked over your whole insides
they'd see that you got a little cancer here
a little diabetes there
there's a clogged artery somewhere
little lumps and bumps nobody knew about
we all got these things
you can't escape it

there's cancer in the food
your house has cancer
your car
the water has little cancers swimmin around in it
there's even cancer in the air!
so what're you gonna do
stop breathin?

if to stop the thing that's killin you
is gonna kill you
what's the use?

i quit smokin doctor

oh good

very very good

so now i leave the doctor's office
and i get run over by a cab
i never make it home alive
i quit the wrong thing
maybe i should've quit walking!

the newspaper says

Deaths

MRS. SO-AND-SO
was 91 years old. She
died of natural causes.

WHAT'S HIS NAME
was 89 years old. He
died of cancer.

i gotta laugh

how about my buddies who got killed in the fuckin war
eighteen nineteen years old they got killed by bullets
i'm sure they would've loved to die of cancer at eighty-nine
they lost sixty years of their life!
he didn't die of cancer
he was eighty-nine years old!
he died when he was supposed to die!

today they got heart transplants
        lung machines
        kidney machines
        pacemakers
        bone marrow transplants
        that's the biggest farce in the world!

everything that lives dies

joe shmo has a heart attack
so they give him another heart
some plastic piece of shit
then one lung collapses
so they give him somebody else's lung
then he has a stroke
so they put a monkey's brain inside his head
they say

> *we saved his life*
> *he lived an extra six months*

big fuckin deal
half a million dollars
goes straight to the
insurance companies
and the hospitals
the doctor gets a new heater
for his swimming pool
if that's progress
you can go fuck yourself!

if i put a beer on the bar and i don't drink it right away

it dies

the bee that stung you last summer

he died

them tombstones out in the cemetery — those people

all dead!

we got just a short time in this life
and most of it is spent worryin about dyin

> *how* am i gonna die?

> *when* am i gonna die?

> *why* am i gonna die?

> *where* am i gonna die?

some people
for ninety years they worry about dyin
what good is it gonna do you
if you're afraid to live
cause you're scared to death of dyin?

don't give me none of that shit
you gonna start readin packages now
what the hell are you readin?

just eat it!

if it comes from the earth then you gotta eat it
cause we're earthlings
you wanna read?
go to a bookstore
you wanna eat?
go to a market
don't talk to me about chemicals
what's wrong with preservatives?
you wanna open up a can and eat mold?
be my guest
you wanna eat bacteria?
go ahead

if this was homemade bread
i couldn't leave it lay here for a week
it has to go on ice
that's why they came up with somethin to preserve it
so we don't get sick
now you're tellin me
what they put in there to preserve it is killin me

get the hell outta here!

i was cookin bacon'n eggs the other day
and nicole says
you ought to be careful about
eatin too many eggs
cause of the cholesterol

i was raised on milk
butter and eggs
eggs are good for you!
you don't die from eggs!
if i wanna have bacon'n eggs for breakfast
a ham'n egg sandwich for lunch
and put eggs in my meatballs tonight
nothin's gonna stop me
my mother always told me

> *eat your eggs*
> *they're good for you*

everything that lives dies

after i came home from the hospital at twelve years old
i wanted to call the nurse for every little ache and pain
that's what i was used to!
but then my mother showed me a different way
no matter what ailments we had
pneumonias
flues
headaches
my mother put her own remedies all over us
mustard
kerosene
raw potatoes
garlic poultices
all kinds of things she used to heal us
and they worked!

today people run to doctors for everything
and what do the doctors do for you?
first they break your balls
then they give you prescriptions for sugar pills
then they throw you out on the street

so you pick your butt off the sidewalk
and crawl over to the drugstore
with fifteen pieces of paper in your hand
the pharmacist takes the little white sugar things
with peppermint
the the the . . .
the tic tacs!
empties all of them into prescription vials
puts little labels on them

> *two hundred dollars please*
> *so long*

you take a coupla those five-cent tic tacs
look in the mirror and say
ming!
i'm all better
but before the week is out
your mind starts workin on some other little thing
your little pinky toe hurts

so you go back to the doctor
he listens to your heartbeat
he checks your blood pressure
you stick out your tongue
he shoves the light up your nose
and gives you another prescription for sugar pills
if you keep comin back to the doctor every ten minutes

complainin and complainin
they'll run you through the test mill
they'll give you every test they can think of
look at me:

    i took the g.i. series
    i took the fluoroscopes
    the spinal taps
    the x-rays

and after all they put you through
all of those tests and machines
and high-class contraptions
after takin all of your money
they still call you a hypochondriac!

fuck the doctor

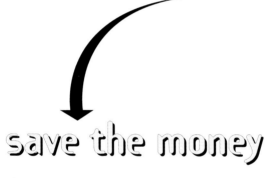

save the money

the only time you go to the doctor is
    • if your heart stops
    • or if the red stuff comes out

stop the bullshit now!
live
work hard
be nice
enjoy yourself
don't do nothin bad to nobody
 and remember
  the agonies
    the ugly aches and pains of life
      is while you're walkin around on this earth
        so get used to it
          and stop complainin!

a capitalist society

any way they can make dough ray me
they'll make it
if they gotta skin cats
and sell dead pet fur
they'll do that too
somebody'll buy it
i told you a hundred times
about this goddamn capitalist society

try this experiment:

- go into the bathroom and take a crap

- then put a little piece in a dixie cup

- do a coupla dixie cups like that

- now go get a box

- put a sign on it that says

FOR SALE

35¢

2 FOR 50¢

5 FOR $1

- then sit out on the corner and see what happens

alotta people won't go for it
most people won't
but if you stand out there long enough
eventually . . .
some schmuck will come along

and buy that crap from you
somebody'll actually buy it!

three million people will pass you right by but one person will finally buy it!

and after a coupla people see that that guy's got one
more people will come around
so then you can raise the price to a dollar a cocky
then five dollars a cocky
after a while you'll be able to hire other people
to work for you
maybe you'll branch out
and start a franchise of cocky stands
then soon you'll be all over the country
but you better make sure to put some of that money away
cause as soon as you can say *poopa scoopa*
some other guy's gonna take a leak
and put it in a cup
and set it up on a little box on the corner
and before you know it
he's the next big thing
and
  you're
    on
      a
        long
          line
            waitin
              to
                pick
                  up
                    your
                      unemployment
                      check

the rise and fall of the union

i

n the beginning
the union came from the people
cause they were gettin ripped off
first thing they did
they fought for wages
benefits and safety
the fat cats said **no way**
so the unions closed em down and that showed em
the next thing the unions did
was to break everything down into groups
you're in group one ☞ this is your job
when the stuff comes in off the truck
you deliver it all through the building
☞ you you're group two
group three ☞ you go out
on the shipping deck
☞ another guy's group five
he does something else
group six ☞ you go there and do x y and z

30 HOUR WEEK

as the years go by management gets to thinkin . . .
THIS GUY IN GROUP SIX HAS TIME ON HIS HANDS
LET HIM HELP OUT THE GROUP TWO GUY
see . . .
they don't want you standin around idle
so they try that on the group six guy — right?
but the group six guy's been around
he goes straight to the union screamin and yellin
but by this time the union's in good with management
it's a fuckin tag team now!
the group six guy tries to put up a fight with the union
but the union man says
                there's nothin we can do about it
all of a sudden he's usin words like
                productivity
                attrition rate
                new quota ratios
                downsizing
                all these high-class words

each union had a different way of dealin with management
my union at The New York Times
sold out to givebacks and layoffs
but the unions upstairs were strong
they stuck up for their rank and file
when everything switched over from metal to cold type
they tried to get rid of all these old linotype operators
(you know — the guys who make the slugs outta lead)
but the union said

**no way
you can't just get rid of them**

they had guys walkin around doin nothin
makin forty thousand a year
didn't retrain em or nothin

eventually when they got these high-speed presses
all the guys had to do was set up the buttons
go hang out in the men's room and play cards

little by little they bought alotta people out
and never replaced em
i missed a buyout myself by about two years
they were givin out severance pay
plus fifty thousand dollars
alotta guys jumped for that kind of cash

so after they get rid of all the people on the floor
who actually do things with their hands
who do you got left?
besides management and middle management
who's left in the work force?

the **answer** :

the engineers

what do they do?
the engineers invent new robots
they invent computers and robots
the robots run the computers which run the factories

you also got the lawyers and the accountants
what do they do?
they tell management to
declare bankruptcy
they file chapter eleven
when that happens
the union doesn't have a leg to stand on

the rise and fall of the union

the workers are out on the unemployment line
for the first time in their lives!
the creditors don't get paid
but the company keeps on makin money on top of money
the v.p.'s are laughin all the way to the bank
they're openin up new plants in thailand
russia and mexico
where they don't got unions to protect the people
meanwhile in this country everybody's losin their jobs
so nobody can afford to buy nothin
and who gets blamed for all the problems?

the unions!
so next thing you're just happy if you got a job
any job!
and then eventually . . .
a union will come up from the people
   cause the people are gettin ripped off
      and the first thing they'll do is fight for wages
         benefits and safety
            and the fat cats will say **no way**
               so then . . .

good advice

you gotta be carefu

if you're white
and you kill somebody who's black
you're in trouble
if you're black
and you kill someone who's white
same thing
you can f'get about it

who you kill today

if you gotta kill somebody
kill somebody who's the same color as you
or else everybody's gonna make
a big to-do about it
thousands of people are gettin murdered every day
all over the country
whites are killin whites
and blacks are killin blacks
nobody seems to care
but if one kills the other
it's all over the papers
and once that happens
you're dead

i find it awful hard sometimes god

god . . .

psst . . .
psst . . .
god . . .
it's me again
nicky d. (the one from l.i.c.)

i gotta talk to you for a second
cause you know i believe in you
i believe in you more than i believe in
just about anything else

but sometimes god
it gets kinda hard down here
cause these times i'm livin in
and all the things i been through
make it hard to tell you're really there sometimes

what i'm tryin to say is
god . . .
i just wish sometimes that you would give me
more of a sign
like
well
when i was young
i believed anything anybody told me
that's the way i am by nature
i'm a libra and libras are trusters
(you know that)
but now that i'm a seventy-two-year-old chicken plucker
i'm not like that anymore
i've been told all kinds of stories in my day
and alotta them turned out not to be true

now i don't want you to take this in the wrong way
cause i don't doubt you and all of what you've done
i never ever doubted you
but since i never got to see any miracles
and things like that myself
how am i supposed to believe in them things
they say you did thousands of years ago in the bible?

like i'm supposed to believe that you made
a talking snake to tempt eve
and you warned noah before you made the forty-year flood
and sent a ladder from heaven into jacob's dream
and manna down from heaven
and turned water into wine
and parted the red sea
and all them other things
i'm supposed to believe
just from readin it in a book
written in english printed in korea!

i'm askin you god
how am i supposed to believe that you had a son
and you sent him to this earth
and his name was jesus christ
and he could make blind people see
and crippled people walk
and raise lazarus from the dead and all of that
and then you let them nail
your one and only son to the cross
and then you resurrected him
after he'd been dead for three days
and . . . and . . . i uh
i've always believed in all them things
i want to believe in all them things
but how do i know they're not just

just

stories

am i supposed to
believe all this on faith?
why can't i see some of them things
with my own two eyes?
can't you give the people of today
half a chance?

i find it awful hard sometimes god

cause if i was walkin down forty-second street
and i seen them draggin jesus
with a cross on his back down greenpoint avenue
sure i'd feel compassion!
especially cause he was supposed to be your son
and cause he was a hebrew
and they were gonna crucify him
and besides if he was alive in my time
i would've seen some of them miracles
with my own two eyes

like the loaves and the fishes
and how he saved mary magdalene
from the throngs and turned her from a hooker into a saint
or if i could go out to long island and see moses
part the long island sound in two
and watch all the jewish people who live out there
walk across to connecticut
or turn a staff into a serpent or somethin
that's all i'd need!

people talk about martin luther king
kennedy
gandhi
they were alright
they did good things
but they were flesh'n blood like me!
and i don't believe in flesh'n blood
i wanna see miracles that no flesh'n blood could do!
then you got me two hundred percent!

listen god
i know that ain't what faith is all about
waitin for a miracle to happen all the time
adele says
> *every day is a miracle*
> *every thing is a miracle*
i say
what the fuck are you talkin about?
she says
> *this is a miracle*
> *the bubblegum is a miracle*
> *the t.v. changer is a miracle*
> *the tissue box is a miracle*

everything she thinks is a miracle!
i don't understand what jews believe in
they got a funny idea that everything is a miracle
i know you ain't no garbage can — god
i know you ain't nothin flesh'n blood can ever even imagine
so why can't i just live with that?
what's wrong with me god?
i gotta see a miracle like moses comin down
with the ten commandments in his hands

the actual ten commandments!

now don't get me wrong . . .
i try my best to live by them ten things
but god . . .
i don't think there's one living human being
on the face of this earth
that could keep them ten commandments
cause you gave moses such ten things
that nobody could actually keep
you know what i think probably happened?
the minute moses came down with them ultimatums
right away all the connivers got their wheels turnin
like you said

> THOU SHALT NOT COVET THY NEIGHBOR'S WIFE

so right away some conniver went next door
and started humpin his neighbor's wife

BOOM
BOOM
BOOM

> THOU SHALT NOT STEAL

boing
ZING

clobber some guy over the head
take his wallet

> LOVE THY NEIGHBOR AS THYSELF

fuck you
lend me a hundred dollars

ain't got it

BANG ...ugh plomp

you must be dyin up there
how bad people have been with them commandments

i find it awful hard sometimes god

which is why i'm thinkin that maybe this is a good time
(if you don't mind me
makin a little recommendation god)
maybe now's one of those special times
when you have to allow the people to experience
some kind of high godly stuff
just some little miracle
one or two little miracles
cause it's gettin pretty bad down here god
this is satan's paradise here
everybody's workin for mr. s.
you gotta do somethin . . .

can you hear me god?

are you with me god?

don't you think things're gettin
just a wee bit outta control down here?

we need help!

all anybody can go by today is the scriptures
and that's nothin but secondhand
don't get me wrong
i'm for your word
your word!
but i can't go to church on sundee
and read words out of a prayer book
that's all flesh'n blood stuff
i can't worship a preacher if he gets up in the morning
and goes to the bathroom
and makes sausages'n eggs
if i can take a razor blade and go
SHLING
SHLING
SHLING
and he bleeds
like the rest of us mortals here on earth
then i can't worship him!

but if i cut him
and no blood came out
i'd fall on my knees
kiss his feet
and ask for spiritual guidance
i would!
i swear i would!

no more offtrack betting
no more smokin cigarettes
it would be the happiest day of my life
cause i would've finally seen
a miracle!
that's what i need god
no priests
no popes
nobody walkin on the face of the earth
just one sign
one small little miracle

don't get me wrong
god . . .
you know i believe in you
don't you?
miracle or no miracle
  i'll always believe in you
      you know that god
          don't you?
              you know that
                  don't you?

65th birthday

what a shame
they bought me a big beautiful cake
with them lousy ugly numbers on it

i went through withdrawal for a year
after lookin at that friggin number
i hated it when i saw that number!
that's an ugly number
cause you know what that number means?

senior citizen
that's what it means!
i hate them ugly friggin numbers
everybody always asks
how old are you?
how old are you?

what the hell's the difference?
they shouldn't have no ages at all!
now i'm seventy-two
and i'm still doin things i was doin when i was nineteen
i see other people my age
they're all crippled up
they're always sayin
don't do this and don't do that
they can go fuck themselves
if you take care of your muni
(that's short for immune system)
and keep in shape
 and don't get hit by a cab
   you can do anything you want
     till you drop to the floor
        and your heart don't beat no more
              age don't mean nothin to me
                it don't mean nothin!

when life leaves you

one religion says

> *first you go here*
> *and then you go there*
> *and blah blah blah blah blah*

another religion says

> **no**
> **first you go over there**
> **then you turn into this**
> **if you were good you go over here**
> **if you were bad you go over there**

who on earth knows what happens to you after you die?

i saw this show last night on channel 5
they had people on who had near-death experiences
    this one lady said

> i ain't scared of dyin no more
> cause i seen death
> and it's a very peaceful thing
> this life here is like a waitin station

she shouldn't say a thing like that on t.v.
cause you're liable to pick up the newspaper
the next morning and read

A HUNDRED MILLION PEOPLE HEARD THAT DEATH WAS A NICE PLACE AND JUMPED OUT THE WINDOW

i don't wanna be president no more
i'd rather be dead **BOOM**
        splat

i don't wanna work in the post office no more
    BANG BANG plomp

then the worms and snails will be runnin the earth
nah nah nah nah nah nah nah
that's no good
this may be just a pit stop
but it's our pit stop
god put us here for somethin
and we've got to do that till it's our time to leave

take a look at the crucifixion story
most catholics say that christ had himself
nailed to the cross so our sins could be forgiven
i think that's bullshit
we're still sinnin more than ever
i say christ allowed himself to be scourged
and crucified on the cross in order to
put the fear in us that

death is bad

everyone could see for all time
the nails goin right through the skin
the blood — the crown of thorns
people see all them pictures of christ on the cross
they think of dyin
they think death is bad
death is horrible
when i was a little kid goin to catholic school
that scared the daylights outta me
christ figured

> IF THE PEOPLE OF THE EARTH KNEW
> THE REAL TRUTH THAT
> DEATH IS A PLEASANT THING
> THEY'D ALL WANNA KILL THEMSELVES

all we mortals have to go on are little glimpses
hints that there's more out there
than we can see with our own two eyes
there's more than flesh and blood and buildings and cars
and cigarettes and all the coffee in the world

the ordinary workin guy just thinks
i gotta get to work
make money
they're the soldier ants!
if they can't put it in their mouths
or in their bank accounts
they ain't interested
the only ones who're interested are the ones who had
strange outta body things happen to them
like me

when life leaves you

we all got our time to go
no sooner — no later
and when that time comes
i'll tell you what i think happens:

at that moment when your breath stops
or whatever the hell you wanna call it
your heart stops
when all that there is gone
and there's no more **ba boom**
ba boom
ba boom
ba boom
there's no more blood circulatin
no digestion
no nerve responses
no thought waves
no more fartin
belchin
laughin
cryin
sneezin
coughin
no more feelin all the little aches and pains
when there's no more childhood memories
no more family parties
no more seein your sisters and brothers
no more goin out and buyin little presents
for your nieces and nephews
when you can't see nobody and nobody sees you

when you don't have any more friends comin to visit
on the spur of the moment
no neighbors droppin in no more
and you can't just throw your favorite videotape
into the v.c.r.
when there's no more eatin
cause you don't have no more taste buds
not for veal parmesan
pizza
broccoli rabe
chocolate
nothin
when you can't taste a thing
you can't smell
you can't see
you can't touch
you can't feel nothin
you can't remember nothin

you can't even forget nothin
when everything that makes you you is gone
and all that's left of you is just a stiff old piece of meat
well . . .
just before that happens
that's when the spirit takes off . . .

sssshhhhhooo

by the time the doctors say
you're dead
the spirit's gone
you just go like that — gently
by the time they tag you
send you to the morgue
your spirit's already on its voyage
it shoots straight into the atmosphere
and just keeps travelin and travelin
till it's approached by whoever's in charge
that's when you get your next assignment
you see all them stars up in the sky?
well i'm sure it's a case by case situation
but as far as the flesh and blood and bones are concerned
poo
that's gone — finished
ninety-eight cents worth of chemicals — that's all
whether you died in some fancy hospital ward
or out in the desert somewhere
your bones turn to dust
and who the hell knows . . .
the dust flies all around
the wind blows the dust onto
a patch of flowers somewhere
and some little kid pulls one of the flowers
outta the ground and brings it home
and then maybe . . .
the mother puts it into a glass of water
and sets it up on the window sill
who the hell knows

what the fuck are we talkin about?
i don't have the time
to bullshit with you all day
i got a roast burnin in the oven
jesus christ!

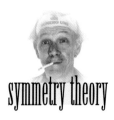

symmetry theory

some guy walks into a high-rise building
takes the elevator up to the top floor
fifteen
sixteen stories up to that little room on the roof
opens the window
and throws a bottle of beer straight down

now the chances of that bottle
hittin somebody on the head are
a million to one

but look at that poor little girl up in the bronx yesterday
walkin down the street mindin her own business
eatin a piece of pizza with her grandmother
and some motherfucker throws a bottle of beer
out the window
and hits her right square on top of the head
she was completely comatose!
they took her in for brain surgery
but it was no use

think of the odds against a thing like that happening:

the building . . . .
                           . . . . the bottle
    the girl . . . . . .
                . . . . . . the grandmother
      the pizza . . . . .
              . . . . . the ground
        the bottle . .
          . . the grandmother
         the pizza . .
         the bottle
         the girl
         and

BING

      right square
    on top of her head
the whole cranium was cracked up bad

if it hit her shoulder first
and ricocheted off her knee or somethin
maybe she'd be alright
just get some little cuts or bruises
maybe even some broken bones
but since it landed on that particular spot on her brain

she's dead

horrible
horrible right?
but . . .
just at that moment
somewhere in a hospital in brooklyn
a new little baby girl was born

that's the way things happen!

you wake up one morning
have breakfast
kiss your wife good-bye

see ya tonight honey

later in the afternoon
the phone rings
your wife picks it up
sorry to have to tell you this ma'am
but your husband's dead
he got hit by a cab

BING

meantime
across town
some other lady meets a guy
and falls in love

all things have their time attached to em
all things have a place
when those two scorecards converge

somethin happens

some people call it an accident
some people call it coincidence
some people say it's luck
some people say it's all in the stars
to me it's just the way things happen
and whatever happens
people either praise god or blame god

symmetry theory

when i was just a little kid
i lost a baby brother
when that baby was born dead
that made no sense to me
i cried and cried and cried
why me?
    why him?
        why us?
i cried when they told me i had osteomyelitis
why me?
   why me?

i cried when i had my first operation
when all the other kids could run around and play
and i had to grow up inside a hospital
why'd my father have to die?
 why this?
   why that?

the answer :  you can't explain it

if you live
you have to see every kind of thing there is
there's no escapin it
i don't care how rich you are
if you live
        you have to see weddings
        you have to see divorces
        parties
        you have to see catastrophes
        you have to see healthy babies
        sick babies
        good movies
        bad movies
        i don't care how much money you have
        there's always bill collectors chasin after you
        no matter who you are
        you're gonna fall in love
        your heart's gonna break at least once or twice
        who can escape a broken heart?

                there's good

there's evil
        that's the way it's always been
        one balances the other

god created the earth with imperfections
he meant for there to be crime
he made criminals
he made cops to arrest em
everybody's got their little part to play

you know there's only

a 25,000 mile

circumference

to
this
piece
of
dirt
we're
on

and besides it's seven-eighths water
if it wasn't for all them things that kill
we'd be climbin all over each other
that's the way it works
half of the world is cryin
the other half is laughin
then it switches around
next week
they're cryin and you're laughin
the sun's shinin over there
it's snowin over here
everybody can scream and yell
it isn't fair
it's the end of the friggin world
till we all got laryngitis
it'll always be like this
till we burn up the earth once and for all
and give another planet a chance

when one door closes

another one opens right up

the final frontier

president kennedy said
we're going to the moon

so we went to the moon
and that's only 200,000 miles away
f'get about it
the moon is close
it's not even ten trips
around the earth
the moon is right here
the sun is 93 million miles away
and look what it's doin to our skin
with the radiation!
the creator made the sun
stay 93 million miles away
otherwise if it was any closer
we'd already be just another
swiss cheese planet

ooooh
what's on mars?

ooooh
what's on jupiter?

ooooh
what's on pluto?

the **answer**:
there's nothin up there
there ain't even air

now they found a coupla more dead rocks
flyin around jupiter
big deal
listen they were just like us
trillions and skillions of years ago
green trees — nice
birds singin
they had all of that
why the hell else did god put them things up there for?
they're shaped like us and everything!
whatever civilizations were on them things
did just what we're doin now!
and then the big explosions came
and destroyed all of them
and now it's our turn
we're the last frontier

in another thousand . . .
     another million . . .
       maybe another thousand million years
        we'll become just another dead rock
        give somebody else a turn
        one by one an old planet dies
        and a new planet comes up
        that's the way it works
        that's the way it's always worked
       this is the biggest secret around
      them son of a bitch scientists
     won't tell you about that
    they wanna keep their jobs
   they wanna spend more of the taxpayers' money
to shoot people up in space
for what?
for what?
to get some fries and a milkshake?

no!
you can't even get
a bottle of coke up there
it's dead — dead!
seven-hundred-mile-an-hour winds
no gravity
they have to wear
three hundred pounds of garbage
if they take it off they die
there's no oxygen up there!

it's fine to look up at the sky and say

ooooh look what god did!
look what god did

the
n
o
r
t
h
e r n   l i g h t s
o
o
t
i
n g
h
s

beeeauteeeful!

that's all
stay here and sing songs about it
(the moon in june
racing with the moon
the cow jumped over the moon
and all of that)
this is our time!
this is earth's time!
those things up there
are made for us
to romance on
kissin and mushin it up in the rumble seat

t a r s

one day a thousand years after the earth
finally destroys itself from evil
and becomes just another dead planet
someone or something
from some faraway planet
(let's call it planet x)
will send space probes to a place called earth
and the leader of planet x
will probably give a speech to his creatures sayin
ask not what i can do for you . . .
blah blah blah blah blah . . .
and they'll waste all their time and money
  shootin rocket ships into space
        and the whole thing will just keep repeatin itself
            over and over and over again

madness

madness?

madness?
what the fuck is that?
everybody has a little madness i suppose
you can't get through life without it
sooner or later it can take hold of you
no matter who you are
it can grab you at any moment

when a husband and wife argue

it's madness

go to the bar and drink all night

that's madness

take your pay
go down to the track and lose the whole thing

that's madness

brothers and sisters refusin to talk

total madness

have a crazy mixed-up dream
wake up
don't know where you are
what's real?
what's not?

that's madness

talk to yourself all day long
watch pictures on the walls come to life
pray to a god you never seen
try to live in peace in a city with eight million people

all them things
are madness

so what are you gonna do
 lock everybody up and throw away the key?
  f'get about it
     just keep your thoughts to yourself
        stick to your own people
           stay inside as much as you can
               and don't talk to too many strangers

on the couch and by the pool

with
family
and
friends

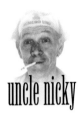

uncle nicky

i got thirty-five nieces and nephews
that's my job now

i'm an uncle!

that's what i am

everybody's got a role in life
some people are parents
some people are presidents
some people are movie stars
some people are writers

i'm an uncle

that's my role
i got put here for a reason
not to have my own
but to take care of **all**
i live for **all**
my nieces and nephews

if i had my own kids
i never would have lasted
i'd be in jail or dead or somethin
cause as long as they were in my cave
they'd have to do as i say
after they grew up
then i'd let them loose into the jungle

the more i think about it
the more i think
it's a good thing my marriage didn't work out
cause if i had kids
someone probably would've ended up bein killed

i'm not kiddin!

even with my nieces and nephews
i get too involved sometimes
i try to interfere with everybody's problems
up until a coupla years ago i was everybody's uncle
everywhere i went i was

uncle nicky!

even with the girl next door i was uncle nicky
i meddled in on everybody's problems

but then it backfired on me
i cared too much
i made their problems my problems
and people don't listen
like when victoria's boyfriend put eight hundred down
on an engagement ring
i told her
please
think it over
don't get stuck again!

i already gave her away once three years ago
she's only a baby
twenty-seven years old
i told her
you're so pretty
you don't have to settle down for a while
wait till you get a little older
have some fun!

she didn't listen to me
(now she's pregnant)
most people don't listen
and that gets me upset

so all i do now is just try to help
i don't interfere
i'm a phila . . . phila . . . phila
philanthropist
can't pronounce the word
can't even spell it
but that's what i am
i set up bank accounts for all my nieces and nephews
every time i win a little money on a bet
i make a deposit
PLINK
        PLINK
            PLINK

i work their gardens
stain their decks
build fences
throw birthday bashes
bake cakes
i do all of that!
but when it comes to givin out advice
i figure
    hey
    i'm seventy-two years old

uncle nicky

you wanna fuck yourself
you wanna shoot yourself
in the foot
leave me alone
if you wanna take my advice
i'll give you some
that's all
i don't interfere anymore
things turn out the way they're meant to turn out

an uncle!
that's what the lord almighty wanted me to end up bein
on christmas i play with all my nieces and nephews
i make em all laugh
better than any comedy you could see on t.v.
they're all on the floor laughin
they love me
 i love them
   i give em little things
     cook for em
        make up crazy games
           things like that
                 then i say **bye-bye**
                 and close the door behind me

the single life

i don't go out on no dates
what for?
i don't want sympathy from no one
i thrive on isolation

they tried to fix me up with some blimp from the bronx
i was dancin with her
she was singin in my ear
squeezin me
she kept on squeezin me
after a while i got scared
she was gonna crush me to death on the dance floor
she was holdin me so friggin tight
i couldn't breathe!
i said to myself
i gotta get the hell outta here

then some other lady grabs me
and wants me to do the lindy with her
i swear they were killin me
i was jumpin around all night like a rabbit
i didn't get to eat till late
my skinny legs don't want to do it no more!
that stuff knocks me out
i'm up there dancin — socializin
tryin to have a good time
and all i keep thinkin about is
me bein back in my own place
 with my feet up on the table
    watchin an old katharine hepburn movie
        suckin on a russell stover chocolate

anyway i don't go out for girls my age
(i don't go for old ladies)
and the young ones don't wanna be hangin on the arm
of an old vampire like me
besides . . .
there are no more
beautiful girls to be had!

ringo starr
that big fat ugly fuck
kick him in the balls
and all the rest of them rock stars
i can't believe he's got such a beautiful wife
i don't know what she sees in him
all these guys that sing and play guitars
and scream and holler up on a stage
who marries em?

the **answer** : all these gorgeous models
and miss americas
all the actresses and beauty queens
they marry em!

then these nice girls get all screwed up with drugs
and demented lifestyles
i don't know what they see in these bastards
who scream their guts out on t.v.
valerie bertinelli married one of em
that other nice russian model
pauline somethin or other
she married one of them ugly singers
these singers get all the great girls!
they're destroyin all the beautiful women on the earth
it's a shame
a cryin shame

middle man

this was a really bad spring
it should've been great!
we had weddings
a christening
two graduations
birthday parties
anniversary parties
retirement parties
one week after the other
you'd think it would've been a great spring!
but it was terrible
one half of the family's not talkin to the other

and i'm stuck in the middle

ever since the big fight broke out at philomena's wedding
my whole family split in two
there's two war zones
one sister still ain't talkin to my other sister
the cousins wanna kill each other
the bride and the groom are mad at that side
and that side is mad at this side
my brother refuses to acknowledge my nephew's new wife
one aunt doesn't talk to one of her three daughters

and i'm stuck in the middle

i talk to everybody and they all talk to me
(except for my sister annemarie
she's the only one who refuses to talk to me
her and tommy)
everybody else comes to squawk with uncle nicky
about their troubles
the only thing is
one side never talks to me about the other side no more

in the beginning they'd slip in little questions
in the middle of a conversation just to find out things
but now nobody seems to care
each side acts like the other don't exist
they either don't wanna know
or they're bitter

the only exception is
everybody wants to know about
the newborn infants
cause when it comes to babies
all the hate and venom disappear
everybody goes ga ga
everybody wants to see pictures of the newborns

the family bullshit is nothin new
it's been like this all through the ages
when we were growin up
my mother used to say

> *don't talk to that aunt*
> *cause she did this to me*
> *and that uncle is no good*
> *and that one's no good*

so you grow up all through life
knowin how to detour certain people
uh oh
here comes aunt so'n so
watch out
there's cousin what's his name

i don't believe in takin sides no more
it tears me up inside to see the family all split up
 so now i'm the middle man
  i want everybody to love everybody
     that's all i want
        i just want everything to be nice
           that's all i want

i'm a city kid

spent the weekend in the country
out on the island with my nieces and nephews
for my birthday
they threw me a party out there
what fun
shhhooooooo
f'get about it
spinach farms
as far as the eye can see
all the way past port jefferson
what a beautiful place!
spinach has got to be the strongest vegetable in the world
even this time of year you can see
miles and miles of spinach
they still use pickers for pickin the spinach
it's not just automated those farms
they got potato farms out there
long island potatoes
fifty pound bags — three bucks
and tomatoes
you should see those tomatoes
they're not like those artificial ones they sell in the city
the tomatoes they got out there are really red
they're real tomatoes
anything you want they grow out there
pumpkin fields all over the place
and moss farms they got
i went to look at how they grow moss
ever seen how they grow moss?
unbelievable!
big long fields
smooth as a pool table
spread out in every direction
i swear to god
you could put a level on that ground
and it'd come up flat
it's like you're lookin at a giant piece of green paper
unbelievable!
they sell the stuff to the lawn companies
and to the ballparks
oh — and the cornfields they got out there!
you should see the farmers
ridin these big tractors they use now

it goes underneath the soil
brings it up and flips it back
bud di de doo
    bud di de doo
        bud di de doo

gina's got this great big pool
the pool's the size of my whole apartment
with all nice tile and everything
beautiful
it's a beautiful place!
jesus
the air out there is so fresh
you could die!

i was standin out in this field one day
trees all around me
nothin but green grass and trees you know
and i'm breathin that nice

        fresh

      pure

    clean

air
and i don't know
if it was killin me or what
but after three days in the country
i started to panic:

what are they tryin to do
clear me all out with all this
nature air stuff?
i can't handle it
there's no noise
nothin
you can hear your heart beat out here
i'm used to the sound of ambulances
and fire engines and car crashes
i'm used to the screeching
decrepit subway cars
and wall-to-wall traffic
and people screamin outside my window
i'm used to the sound of them ugly
alarms goin off all the time

i'm a city kid

i'm used to the smell of garbage
i'm used to the smell of piss
in the alleyways
and the carbon monoxide
and the smoke and the filth
i guess i even got used to mobs
of people tramplin over me
to get to wherever the hell they're goin
fast
faster
i'm used to the fast pace
the zip pe de rop
zip pe de rop
snap snap
next
you're next
get there
get there
bim boom rop
i'm used to watchin out
 for the dirty pimps
    and the drug addicts
       and the muggers
          i'm used to times square
             the neon
                the flashin lights
                   all the beautiful girls

i'm used to walkin to the corner
to pick up my ham'n swiss
and a lottery ticket

i had a nice time out there
 but three days is enough for me man
  i gotta get back to the city
   i can't spend my time
       chasin wild rabbits all day
       i'm a city kid!

bathing suit pictures

this is a picture of my niece gina

—————

this is gina in a two-piecer

—————

this is gina in another two-piecer by the pool in long island

—————

this is my sister nette

—————

there's gina again at jones beach

—————

nydia in a one-piecer

—————

lookit
there's nicole layin down on the betty boop blanket i got her

—————

gina in bayside

—————

gina in l.i.c.
(we used to have a pool in the back next door
coupla years ago)

—————

the lady upstairs sent me this picture of her
from jamaica or trinidad or someplace

—————

here's gina jumping off the diving board

—————

here's donna and victoria at the beach in mt. sinai

—————

victoria in florida
i told her
never stand with your legs apart like that

i told her
**if you're gonna pose for a picture
always close your legs
with the toes pointing out
that makes everybody look perfect**
(girls that just stand there like lumps
look like any kind of homo sapien)

———

here's donna puttin on suntan lotion
i told her
i'm burnin that bikini
(she don't look good with ruffles)
i told her
**get somethin smooth
ruffles just don't work with your figure**

———

gina makin cross-eyes by the pool in bayside

———

these girls are my pinups
i like to look at pretty things
guys are ugly

poo
they stink!
if i had the napalm bomb (the flame thrower)
i'd get rid of all guys
frig guys
i don't bother with pictures of that
hey me too!
i'm the head vampire
me — i'm the ugliest thing walkin the face of the earth
i know what's what

———

this is gina and chrissy with their sun reflectors

———

this is my cousin cecilia by the pool in mt. sinai

———

this is my sister nette last fourth of july

———

this is my . . .

the lady upstairs
written with adele shtern

<u>every day is christmas to her</u>
when i first broke my neck
that lady would come downstairs with a hot water bottle
i just thought that was a million dollars
when i had the flu
she'd ask me if i wanted somethin
she'd make me tea
rub my neck
get my mail
bring me little presents
she's still bringin me presents all the time
she don't surprise me when she buys me
a gift for christmas

every day is christmas to her!
you can't talk in front of that lady
cause i know if i'm talkin to her about somethin
she's puttin it down in her computer
like maybe i'll pick up the t.v. guide and mumble somethin
about wantin to record some movie
but not havin any tapes
or i'll say somethin about some kind of candy i like
then two three days later
she comes back with videotapes
and a coupla boxes of that same candy
most people wait for birthdays
new year's and christmas
it's different with her

<u>mister grey the scoffer</u>
i'm takin care of her cat the scoffer
seven o'clock this morning he was gorgin himself
he needs a lot of food that bum
scoffin and scoffin
what's he think — he's a chow hound?
i think that kitty thinks he's a dirty little doggie
he's so hungry by the time i get there
he just gobbles down the food in two seconds
the dirty little guinea pussycat is a real con artist
you'd think he's a *naplidan*
straight from naples
the way that beast eats

why don't you send your jew friends chanukah cards?
that's what i asked her
    she said

        it's commercial
      i said
        it's not commercial
        it's loving!
        it's caring!
i asked her
        you mean you weren't happy
        when i gave you them cards?
        chanukah's your christmas right?

oh c'mon
i hear her say god bless and talk about miracles
it's the same thing as christmas
what the hell's the sense of havin all them holidays
shanah tovah
rosh hashanah
chanukah
if you can't send no cards?
what does she care if it costs thirty-five cents?
if you pin em all around the house like me
put em on the frigidaire
up on the door
on top of the t.v.
it makes you feel nice
you feel good for a coupla days

that's what
holidays are for!

chanukah like i never known it
you know if you look at them candles long enough
they have a soothing effect
i love them things!

when that lady upstairs does the chanukah ceremony
i get tranquil
i only ever heard rabbis doin it with their ugly voices
i don't enjoy hearin that
when she sings the high and low pitches
it's pleasurable
when i hear her do that
i go right into it
like i'm a jew myself

the lady upstairs

did warren tell ya?
i called him a jew last night
i was teasin him
    i says
        are you a good jew or a bad jew?
        (like i was quotin dorothy in the wizard of oz
        are you a good witch or a bad witch?)
   he says
        a bad jew
i ask him
        is shanah tovah
        the same as chanukah?
he don't know he says
he don't know much about jewish stuff that guy
you know why?

he wants to work his whole life!
that's all he does
he don't give a shit about religion or ceremony
or candles or menorahs like she does
he don't care about that
all he sees is work

ain't you glad?
it come to me adele's been livin upstairs for ten years
i told her
        you live here ten years
        ten years
        you're living in this building already
        ten years
        it seems like ten days!

time to me
is like time to god
five thousand years
can be a matter of an hour

        figure that one out
        if she tells me she's gonna meet me
        at six o'clock someplace
        and i'm there bidin my time
        and then she comes ten minutes later
        that ten minutes
        seems like ten years
        ain't that a funny thing?

professor
i gotta remember to call her professor from now on
what a title
professor adele
that should be worth a hundred-thousand-dollar salary
and up
the salary she's drawin should be just the tax
but that's the way it goes
everybody's scared to open their mouths these days
cause if you complain they'll throw you out
they'll find somebody else
and pay them thirty-five cents an hour

she made me eat the whole pumpkin pie
nobody ate my pumpkin pie
i wound up with the whole thing
last week i had to eat
a whole entenmann's coconut pie
the week before
a whole pot of beef stew
a whole pot of gravy'n meatballs
that lady didn't come down once today
i had to finish all the hot dogs
sauerkraut and baked beans myself
nobody showed up to help me eat
no phone calls
nothin

allergies
what can carrots do to you?
she says she's allergic to carrots
you never seen a blind rabbit did you?
they're good for your eyes
carrots are vitamin A
anything that comes from the ground
has got to be good for you
i told her
stay away from them allergists!
once they know they got somebody hooked
they'll keep em comin for millions of scratches
someday she'll find the right doctor
and he'll say
nah
nah
you're only allergic to yourself!

arthritis

get the hell outta here

that's what i told her
  i don't got any of them diseases
    them things are for old dudes
      i'm not old
        i'm nicky d.

all them painters

that picasso painting went for fifty million dollars
i can't even afford to look at that stuff
picasso
rembrandt
toulouse-lautrec
who the hell are they?
look at their paintings
they stink!
i used to do better than that in 2a at saint mary's school
i asked adele

      you went to art school
      don't you think them artists
      were nothin but bullshit artists
      rip-off artists?

i don't know why they call them famous
them bums painted with cat-hair brushes
in their backyards under a tree
what the hell's the big deal about a vase of flowers?
i look at their paintings
i see a lot of colors there
but i don't see no art
the closer you get to it the more grotesque it looks
cause it's just globs of brush marks
it's nothin but a bunch of scribbles
you gotta view their art from fifty feet away
i don't want that
i wanna be able to go right up to a painting
and see smooth
i want to look at something nice and smooth
solid
no lines in scenes like a t.v. screen
i want solid streaks
that's what i call **real art**
when it looks solid
solid

whatever she wants
i told her
this year the present i'm buyin you
you go buy!
whatever you want
that way there'll be no disappointments
what do you want
some more art supplies?
a headphone set?
whatever you want

i'd really like to get her a new pair of reeboks
the kind that reach right up to the ankles for winter
but she refuses to tell me her size
i don't know how to buy shoes for girls!
(girls' sizes don't make sense to me)
this way if she picks it
she's guaranteed happy

i don't believe in oral sex
i asked her
why would any girl do oral sex?
it's tough enough tryin to kiss a friggin girl
now you wanna do them things
for what reason?
what kind of pleasure do you get from it?

cause to me that's devil's pleasure
god gave you a mouth so you can eat food and stay alive
that's a sick thing for a girl to do!
you got the ammunition to have sex the proper way
you gotta go to another friggin planet
if you wanna do them dirty things

stay here tonight
she had to leave and go jump on a plane
i told her
frig all that travelin around
you're gonna lose all them hours
stay here
yeah
sit with your cats
and your knitting
and me downstairs

change of heart

i'm in the pool
laid out on the rubber raft
in never-never land
takin a snooze out on the water
all of a sudden
the freakin kids
come from behind
(scare me half to death)
pull the raft out from under me

and dump me

so i gotta go and chase em all over
i grab em
hold em under the water
throw em all around the pool
rough em up a little
and that's it
(we have a little fun)

sure
when gina and carlo first bought the house in long island
i didn't like goin out there
i couldn't take being there for more than a day

what do you expect?
i'm seventy-two years in the shittin city
how do you expect me to acclimate
to country livin overnight?
i had to get used to the territory
i had to get used to the good life
it didn't take me long
(two or three weekends)

tell you the truth
it was the pool that did it!
i like bein down at the bottom
i don't do laps
i don't swim
i just dive in and get absorbed by the whole pool
and come up the other side
jump on the rubber raft
take a sun bath

then i dive in again
i'm a deep-sea man
i'm a fetcher — an eel
sometimes i find a nickel or a part of a toy
i get my ears cleaned out down there
sometimes i wish i could stay down there
at the bottom of the pool forever
cause everything's so blue
everything is wet
everything flows
everything feels just right down there

now i'm hooked for life

i'm goin out there every weekend this summer
gina's got a room on the second floor just for me
i got a bureau with some clothes in it
my swimming suit
my barbecue chef's hat
and gardening jeans
they put me to work as soon as i get out there!
last weekend i planted sweet corn
zucchini
carrots
eggplant
basil
and parsley
first thing when i get out there tomorrow
i'm gonna jump on the machine and mow the lawn
i'll mow all the lawns!
cut the grass down nice and low
give em all crew cuts

by the time i get back to the city i need a vacation
it feels good to be in my own palace again
i get to do things in my own way
but then by tuesdee
i start countin down the days till the weekend
wednesdee
 thursdee
  fridee
   then on fridee night
    i wait for the car to honk
     and i'm outta here

no ordinary pictures

i was like most people
most people can only see the things of this earth:
trees
houses
cars
sky
garbage cans
all the normal naked-eye things
but then i got this camera
it was just a cheap 110 instamatic piece of crap
i got for free with some coupons
but it turned out that this camera was

no ordinary picture taker

cause every time i took a picture of my niece gina
it picked up her ECTOPLASM in all the prints
there was ECTOPLASM all around her

everybody's got ECTOPLASM
but it's not the kind of thing that
any normal camera can pick up
the crazy thing is
i took these pictures of gina at random!
i took them at weddings
at parties
outside
inside
it didn't matter

the first time it happened
i shot a whole roll of twenty-four exposures
all different people
when i developed the pictures
all of them were normal except for gina's
every picture of gina had ECTOPLASM
comin right outta her head
and all the way down her shoulders
it was all around her!
i couldn't figure it out
so i bought another roll of film
and told gina to come over to the house with the kids
after we had dinner i took out my camera
and started snappin some shots of the kids
and then i took one picture of gina

when i got the pictures back
sure enough the ECTOPLASM was there
but it was only in the shot of gina

i couldn't understand what was goin on
so i took the pictures to a professional photographer
and i asked him
> ### what the hell is this?
> ### is there light gettin into
> ### the camera or what?

he looked at the pictures a coupla times
> and said
>> *it can't be!*
>> *this camera's just a dollar-and-a-half job*
>> *how can it be this sensitive?*
>> *i don't understand*

> i said
>> ### what is it?
>> ### what is it?

> he says to me
>> *that's no light leak*

> i ask him
>> ### could the film be defective?

> he says
>> *no*
>> *cause they all came out perfect*
>> *except for this one*

so then i showed him all the previous shots
with the same funny clouds all around her
that's when he told me
that it was her ECTOPLASM comin out on the pictures
i laughed so hard
> i says
>> ### now you have to tell me
>> ### what the hell you're talkin about

> he says
>> *if you look in the dictionary*
>> *ĕc-tō-plăsm*
>> *is sort of like a spiritual thing*
>> *like an energy field*
>> *that the human eye can't see*
>> *but it hovers around the body*
>> *all the time*
>> *in an invisible force field*
>> *like an aura*

that's how i found out about ECTOPLASM
from that photographer!

no ordinary pictures

when i came home
i told a coupla people in the family what he said
so they got together and bought me
this new 35 millimeter camera for my birthday
with rapid-fire exposures
and all kinds of special things on it
so i had gina come over
so i could shoot a whole roll of twenty-four shots
continuously

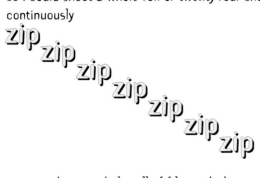

you can shoot a whole roll of film with that camera
in thirty seconds

i was hopin to capture the ECTOPLASM in motion
cause when i got out all the pictures i ever took of gina
i noticed that there were traces of ECTOPLASM
goin as far back as two years!
and in every picture
the ECTOPLASM took on different shapes
different forms

two years ago
gina's ECTOPLASM looked just like an old man
hoverin around her head
then it looked more like a willow tree
and then like a crown
(you know) more like a standard halo

after i did some research into the subject
i found out that ECTOPLASM will sometimes take form
into a shape that mortals can recognize
in order to send out different messages

so i shot two rolls of film with the fancy new camera
with the special speed-mount gizmo

zip zip zip zip zip

but it didn't pick up any of gina's ECTOPLASM
so i went back to the little twilight zone camera
but it didn't ever work again neither

the truth is

i haven't gotten another shot of her ECTOPLASM
in six months
at first i was upset
i tried it with another one-time-shot camera
but it didn't work
so i gave up tryin
to tell you the truth
i don't really need the camera anymore
cause now when i'm with gina
and the light is hittin her in just the right way
i can sorta see her ECTOPLASM
i don't need the camera no more
i can see her ECTOPLASM
with my own two eyes

long island pictures

the house in long island
this is the house
ain't it nice?
that's my room up on the second floor
see the beautiful fir trees
all around the perimeter
other than that it's all open space
nothin but lawn
on one side there's the volleyball net
on the other side (in the back)
there's the pool
look at that pool
ain't it pretty?

terry
the one hidin behind ronnie and carmine
that's gina's other little thing terry
she destroys me
she talks like a twenty-five-year-old girl
she's just two years old!
she's got the mind of a genius
that little thing destroys me
look at her!

carlo
here's a picture of the whole gang
piling up on carlo
they're doin a real job on him
first raymond jumped on top of him
then chrissy jumped on
(i think that's when
she scratched his back)
look — even mossy's barkin at him
(after a while he broke loose
and dived in the pool)

u.f.o.
this is a picture of gina takin a picture of a u.f.o.
you see the u.f.o. flyin over her head?
that strange-lookin thing in the sky
it looks like some kind of weird jet
she just gave me a haircut
and then we went out
and i saw that thing comin right at us
we grabbed our cameras
and took some shots before it passed
we didn't go runnin to the newspapers or any of those shits
cause they would've only made a big media thing out of it
we know what we saw

special shoot
i stood on top of the monkey bars
for about an hour
and shot a whole roll of pictures
of the kids down under me on the swings
i caught em as they were in midair
i liked it so much up there
i told em to send me up a cheeseburger
i'm up there eatin barbecued spareribs
drinkin coke
everything!
i felt like a king

everybody eatin cake
i took the car and drove down to the clearview bakery
and got a big strawberry shortcake
the two fathers like nuts
so i got them a pecan marble loaf
me and the girls wiped out the shortcake
while the nut boys gobbled down the pecan loaf

christiana
i did an experiment with my camera
cause for some reason
every single time i took a picture of chrissy
she came out small
like an insect in the middle of the picture
i look through the camera and there she is
fillin up the whole frame
but after i had the pictures developed
she still came out small

long island pictures

i thought
what the fuck is goin on?
i can't understand it
i like takin pictures of chrissy
so i had an idea:
i took a big magnifying glass and put it
on top of the lens of my camera
snapped a bunch of shots of chrissy
click click click
and sure enough she came out big
focus was nice and sharp
and chrissy was just the right size

first time i seen carlo cleanin out the bug zapper
how the hell can them bugs be so dumb?
to fly into fifteen thousand volts of electricity headfirst
i never seen one of them things before
    i said
what do you got — fireflies?
carlo says
no they're gettin bopped
they're gettin zapped

the first night i stayed over
that machine was goin nonstop
        zzzzzzzip
        zzzzzzzip
        zzzzzzzip
        zzzzzzzip
        zzzzzzzip
            when carlo emptied out
            the tray in the morning
            there were thousands of toasted gnats
            mosquitoes
            flies
            moths
            meanwhile carlo's got mosquito bites
            all up and down his legs
            me i don't have one bite on my body
            bugs don't bother me
            ## i'm poison!
            they know
            if you bite nicky d.
            you die!
            it's in my blood
            i'm my own bug zapper

maryanne
there's that ECTOPLASM again
but this is different than gina's
remember how gina's ECTOPLASM
was cloudy?
how it kinda shrouded around her?
maryanne's ECTOPLASM is different
it's more like a loop shootin down
around her head
somehow i caught it with
the 35 millimeter camera
it had to be comin real strong from her
cause i just used an ordinary flash
maryanne's like a wallflower
she doesn't wanna dance
she's a very shy girl
but she's got good ECTOPLASM
she just doesn't know how to use it

kids: how they get hurt
you know how cold it was outside when i took
this?
it must've been fifty degrees
kids'll swim in friggin ice water
they got no feelings!
they want somethin
they go for it
they don't look where they're goin
if you don't hold their hand
and daddy's over there across the street
they just see daddy
that's all they see
they wanna go to daddy
who cares what's comin across the street
 sherman tanks
   parades
     hurricanes
       that's how they get bopped up all the time
         they live in a twilight zone
                 # they're kids!

trade-off

they'd be givin my brother **lady's tits**
cause he's got prostate cancer
if it wasn't for the x-ray treatments
he'd probably need to start wearin a bra

i mean
they say he's comin along
they say he's doin a lot better
cause . . .
see . . .
he started growin these tits
due to the hormones
so they stopped givin him the hormones
and started givin him the x-ray treatments

now they say
he needs four or five more weeks
of these special x-ray treatments
(where they x-ray your tits before
they put you back on the hormones)
cause if you're a guy
and you take the hormones without these x-ray treatments
then your tits just keep growin and growin
cause it's a female hormone
this is the new technique they got today
whatever they took outta his prostate
 the little piece of shit cancer thing
   got wiped out
      but they still want to finish with the hormones
         to make sure he doesn't ever get any more cancer
            they say once he's finished with the hormones
               he could live forever!

then i got to thinkin that the x-ray treatments
probably give you cancer!
which is crazy cause that's what he had in the first place

tits or cancer

i guess it's a trade-off
seems in life
you always gotta make these tough choices

my sister annemarie is dead

my sister annemarie died this morning
great way to celebrate my birthday huh?
last year on my birthday we got the news — she got cancer
this birthday — she's dead

nine o'clock this morning
i just ate a nice bowl of oatmeal
a soft boiled egg
and some challah bread toast and coffee
i pick up the phone
and my brother tony tells me
i got bad news

i said **uuugh**
the oatmeal and the rest of my breakfast
started rollin around in my stomach
      chi koong
   chi koong
chi koong

then (sure enough) he tells me
our sister died this morning

i haven't seen my sister annemarie for three years
right after philomena's wedding
(after the big fight broke out)
i went up there to visit with her
wish her a happy new year
she tells me
> *i made my new year's resolution*
> *that we shouldn't speak no more*

she tells me she never wants to see me again
she kept to it
i kept my end of the deal too
some people after you tell em to get the hell outta here
i never wanna see you no more
they keep comin around
i'm different!
soon as you look at me crooked
i'm gone
off your computer forever

after a lifetime of always doin things for her
givin and doin and fixin and schleppin
her new year's resolution was never to see me again!

my only regret is
she wouldn't speak to me before she died
she left without speakin to me

the resolution will be kept for all eternity!

now there's chaos on who's gonna go to the wake
they're all afraid there might be more fightin
my sister nette and her daughter gina wanna go
but cecilia (annemarie's daughter) is still very bitter
when she got the news her mother died
i heard she shook like a leaf
even so . . .
she knows how to keep a vengeance
she picks up where her mother left off

me?
i'm definitely not goin to the wake
do i look like a hypocrite?
if i walked in there i'd belittle myself
i'd be the biggest hypocrite on the face of the earth
vinny feels that way too
after throwin bombs and shells at me and daggers all the time how could i go and look at her lyin in a casket?
you know if there were any powers on the earth
she'd get up outta the coffin and start cursin at me again
what good is a brother or a sister or a cousin
when they're dead?
what good are they then?
huh?
the family's got to get together now!
while they're still alive!
have parties
laugh
have fun
not wait around till the ☎ rings

hey guess who died...

my sister annemarie is dead

i hate wakes anyway
i didn't even hang around my own mother's wake
i just don't like them things
it's only chemicals layin there inside that coffin

but everybody likes to get together and weep and moan
do me a favor
don't come to my wake
get together with me now
while i'm still alive!

tony just got back from the funeral parlor sayin
you should see her
they did her up good
she looks like an eighteen year old
she hasn't looked this good in years

none of us even knew annemarie was back in the hospital
nobody called to tell us she was dyin

nette used to go and visit her
the first time she was in the hospital
she brought flowers and things up there
but annemarie just threw everything back at her
(eventually she let her in
screamin and hollerin the whole time
but at least she let her in)
if nette even mentioned my name
annemarie'd go through the roof
i still don't know for what reason!
all i ever did was try to make peace
that's all i did
was try to break up the fight before somebody got killed
and they wind up blamin me for the whole fracas

so here i am alone on my birthday
eatin candy
whoo**pee!**
i told everybody to f'get about it
no use celebratin
(they were all ready to come and have my party anyway
they had all the gifts wrapped up nice
cake and everything)
nette broke down over the phone
cause she couldn't be by her sister's bed at the end
that's bad

there was a time me and annemarie were tight

she's the one who nursed me back
to the land of the living after i quit drinkin
she's the one who lived two blocks away
so we could be near each other
when annemarie was good she was really good
she went all out
but when she was bad she was terrible
she got more closeness off of me than all the rest
i spent so much of my time fixin up her place
doin things for her
till eventually i stopped goin there every night
i started fixin up my own environment
then i got closer to nette and the rest of the family
annemarie might've got a little jealous or somethin
i don't know what it was
but one thing led to another
and then it was nothin but rivalry

**now i'm goin back in my computer
to think what i could've done
to make her so bitter**
i can't think of nothin

every sundee morning
her husband (ron) came down here
i took him to greenpoint to buy groceries
(i never let him pay)
i used to get their traffic summonses here all the time
cause she still used her maiden name and this address
and rather than bug her
i'd go down to the bank and make money orders out
and pay the summonses off myself
one time i seen a letter on the table
says she's behind on her car insurance $380 or somethin
i picked it up off the table
slipped it in my pocket
went down to the bank
got a money order and mailed it out
i did whatever i could
i put up her antenna
fixed her radios
fixed her t.v.'s
built shelves
then all of a sudden
she's mad at me

i don't know
maybe it was one of those little digs
i throw in between conversation

my sister annemarie is dead

i told her one time:
**you know when i do something for adele
she appreciates it
she says thank you
and when i hear thank you
that means my heart gets big
and i get happy
cause i know i did somethin good!
just because i'm your brother
it's oh c'mon fix this
fix that
this is broke
that's broke
i need this
lend me that**

she says
> *nicky
> you gotta do those things for me
> you're my brother*

i didn't say nothin
i just let it go

maybe it had somethin to do with that little problem
she had with her mind when she was younger
when the city hospital gave her shock treatments
maybe that led up to her demise
cause tony just told me the cat scan
found somethin terrible growin inside her brain
which makes me think her mental things
were connected to her dyin
maybe that's why she acted the way she did
the last years of her life
maybe that explains it

once your cancer is diagnosed as terminal
i don't give a fuck what they do to you
cobalt
radium
chemo
radiation
whatever treatment they blast you with
as soon as you hear the word

terminal

you know you only got
twelve to fourteen months left on this earth

(except for jack zippy
after they told him he had terminal lung cancer
they took out one of his lungs
and he's still drinkin and drivin thirty-two years later)

now tony calls me up and wants to know
if i have a picture of mom they can put in the coffin
i says
c'mon what the hell is that gonna do?
(but tony's an old-fashioned guy)
so i said
alright
i'll cut out a little wallet size picture
you can put it in there
annemarie's goin on top of my mother anyway
she might as well have her picture
there's three people under there already
my father
carmella
and my mom
now they're puttin annemarie on top of all them!
what people don't understand about graves
after years and years
those bodies ain't there no more!
every fifteen twenty years or so
you can put another body in there
they just keep carvin more names on the headstone
more names
        more names
more names

annemarie was the last one born and the first one to die
i don't hold no grudge
i know the good times i had with my sister
and those're the times i'll try to remember
not the body
not the tombstone
  not the fights
    and the silences
        the good times!
          that's what i'll try to remember
            the good times!

just in case

i want you to do me a favor
it's no big deal or anything
cause i don't have any problem with . . .
you know . . .
i mean . . .
i'm ready to go right now
if that's what god wants me to do
if he's ready for me

i'm his!
i've had enough of this crazy ass world anyway
believe me
but . . .
just in case . . .
just in case for some reason
if they think i'm dead
i want you to do a little favor for me
just in case they make any mistake
just in case
god isn't really ready for me
i want you to do me a little favor:

you know how
when you hear a song or a record you like
it can make you
like get up right out of a sickbed
and do a dance

and you know how there are certain numbers
and certain singers that sing
like when i was sick with the flu
and i had a 102-degree fever
and barbra (streisand) started singin
somewhere
a place for us
hold my hand and we're halfway there
hold my hand
and i'll take you there

remember how my temperature went
right back down to 98.6?
i mean the way she sings that song makes me
so happy!
and that other song
that jewish song that she sings
they played
the band played that thing at jerry's wedding
that song would make me get outta the friggin grave
it's like a blood transfusion!

they had a lady singer
who should've been playin carnegie hall
she sings italian
she sings *arrivederci roma* in italian

my buddy
the psychiatrist (the italian)
he got chills he liked that so much!
and she sang some puerto rican
and some german songs
mack the knife
whatever
but when she started singin that jewish song
that's when i started gettin that feeling

(to the tune of *hava nagila*)

      la la
        la la la lala
          la la la lala
            la la la lalalalala

    da da
      dat dat da dum
      da da
        dat dat da dum

oh boy
i got off of that friggin seat
in the middle of eatin my steak
and i went and **grabbed** one of the girls
to come and dance with me
i had to do it!
it's like a thing that just gets inside of me
like god is talkin to me
like when glenn miller does *moonlight serenade*
or artie shaw does *begin the beguine*
you know
i sink my mind into that

just in case

and there's no more stinkin time bomb
tickin of the clock
there's no newspaper headlines
there's no ugly landlords
there's no social security checks
no horseshit presidents
there's no life or death
or young or old
there's no senior citizen cards
no hardening of the arteries
there's nothin

for

those

few

minutes

there's

nothin

except

bein

in

the

middle

of

that

there

sound

like when barbra holds a really really long note
you know how barbra (streisand)
can hold her notes to the fullest
that gets me right outta the grave

so before they throw the dirt on me
if you can do me a favor
and make sure they try that
will you?
when they think i'm dead
tell em not to lock the casket

and before they throw the dirt on me
can you make sure to bring out a record player
and put on one of my barbra records
put on barbra singin
somewhere
or **people**
or
or
or that **jewish song**
or somethin
cause
i don't know
you never know
just in case somethin goes wrong
and it's not really my time yet
and
and
i'll make sure you have enough extension cord
or one of them booster battery units
i'll take care of all of that
cause . . .
who knows?

who knows?
if they make a mistake or somethin
it might just do the trick

some famous recipes

just plain french fries

PRODUCE OF U.S.A. *Ingredients*

for normal people	**for hypochondriacs**
idahos	red potatoes
olive oil (100% virgin)	crisco
salt'n pepper	salt'n pepper

i'll show you how i make french fries
but remember
nobody can copy my french fry technique
nobody
so don't even try!

when i'm eatin alone
i don't usually wanna have just plain fries
i make em with onions'n eggs'n pepperoni
sometimes salami
then i add some parmesan cheese on top
i make a big french fry pie out of it
i lock my door and nobody comes in
but most people just want em plain
they put a little salt on
some ketchup
maybe a little vinegar
occasionally i have someone over
who likes em with onions
but this here technique is for those people
who just like their fries **plain**
just perfectly cooked plain french fries

i only use idahos
even though adele says red potatoes give you less arthritis
you think i'm gonna listen to her?
she can scratch her ass with that stuff
if she's comin over then i'll cook with the reds
i got some on my last trip to long island
they grow red potatoes out there
i just stick my hand in the ground
and pull out as many as i want

nowadays
alotta people bitch about too much grease
for them you can use crisco
it comes out drier
but i prefer to use pure virgin olive oil
either way you don't need to use too much
some people deep-fry like they do in restaurants
don't do that
that'll kill you!

this is what you gotta do:
first you skin your potatoes in a circular motion
nobody can explain how to cut a potato
or how to cook a potato
you can't explain it!
you have to feel it
you have to learn through experience
you can't cook outta books
you gotta know the touch
the smell
the people you're cookin for

what you do is you take your knife
and just spiral it down
             spiral it down
        spiral it down towards the thumb
cut whatever you see that you're not gonna eat
some people take a week to peel a potato
all you gotta do is **zip zip zip**

next thing you cut them into slices
schling schling schling schling
not too fat not too thin
i like it somewhere in the middle
first you cut em on the long side
then reverse it the other way
schling schling schling
grab a handful
then hold it tight with your thumb
        then down
           down
      down
   down
      down
make sure you keep em long
don't cut the fries into little nothins
i like to pop a raw slice in my mouth from time to time
we ate raw potatoes when i was a kid
i'll tell you somethin else we used to do with potatoes

just plain french fries

we'd put a flat piece of potato in some cheesecloth
and put it over boils
that was one of my mother's home remedies
if you had a hot-oil burn
she'd put ice-cold potatoes right on the burn
some mothers used butter
but that cooked the friggin burn right in
never use butter
throw your butter out!
butter is no good
on the earth
(the only thing butter's good for is toast)
when you're done choppin up all your taters
put your olive oil in the frying pan — heat it up
take a handful of your sliced potatoes
throw em in the pan and wet em up in the oil
throw a little pepper'n salt in
then rev up the gas (let it get nice and high)
cause they gotta get singed

                              stir

              stir

       stir
then cover your top
keep cookin em
cookin em cookin em
when they start to get golden brown
then you cut the flame down low and let the insides bake
eventually you get a feel for how
the potatoes wanna be done
they're tellin you how to do the flames themselves
just ask em
they know!
when you think the bottom is gettin crispy brown
then you flip em
flip flip flip
flip flip
flip
they're happy in there
you can hear em singin!
listen . . .
they're singin in there
you hear em?

there are two things potatoes hate the most:
  • they hate bein burnt to a crisp on the outside
    and raw on the inside
  • and they hate bein cooked in too much oil

so don't let em get too brown
if the phone rings
you either gotta have a long cord
and be good at doin two things at once
or you gotta tell em you'll call right back

watch out when you lift up the cover
you don't get splashed with hot oil
that's real hot oil in there
it'll hop out all over your face
so be careful!
by the time these babies are cooked
there should be no more oil in the pan
what didn't evaporate got absorbed into the potato
you should be able to just pop em in your mouth
and eat em

this asshole chef in the newspaper
wrote up a recipe for french fries
he calls it thrice fried

thrice fried
my ass

after he cooks em up once he fries em up again
and then again
for what?
why would you wanna do that?
they're gonna go **cook cook cook**
and it'll be **shit shit shit**

my fries are done in one shot
no second chances
as soon as they're cooked
i throw em on the table
that's when you can add that ugly filthy ketchup
with all them spices in there
vinegar
  whatever you want
    even with nothin on them
      most people finish em off
        before you can say french fries

nicky d.'s famous marinara sauce

olive oil (100% virgin)
garlic (bunch of cloves)
fennel seeds
basil (fresh if you got it)
salt'n pepper
a can of tomato paste
a can of whole plum tomatoes
with basil leaves

first get yourself a good pot
no use cookin with a piece of tin
spray some olive oil in the pot
(i use 100% virgin cold pressed)
put the flame on low so you don't let it burn
while you mince up some fresh rhinoceros garlic cloves
big ones!

some of the housewives take the shortcut
they take the garlic
and they smash it with the side of a big knife
no good no good!
you can't smash the garlic
it goes into shock
you don't wanna eat shock
you wanna eat finesse!
get your favorite sharpest little knife
slice the garlic as thin as possible
usin your fingernails as a guide
so you don't cut your hand
slide off the fingernails
slide
CUT
slide
CUT

most people won't cut garlic this way
cause they're afraid they'll cut themselves
which they will if they're sloppy

never use a garlic press neither
you lose all the juices

punch up all the garlic and scrape it into the hot oil
raise your flame a little till it's golden brown
smear it around in the pan
till it gets cooked up nice and even

now . . .
open your kitchen window
and let the smell of the garlic go outside
so all the neighbors can come down
and ask to have dinner with you
yeah!

then lower your flame back down as low as you can
open up a can of paste (hunt's tomato paste)
take the paste and throw it in the hot oil
and just feel those little hot drips goin all over your body
a normal person would be jumpin and screamin
but after all these years it don't bother me

use a spatula or a spoon to get all the paste outta the can
now go over to the sink
and fill up the can with water (halfway)
blend the leftover paste in with the water
blend it down nice
and pour that into the pot
keep the flame very low
cause once it starts to bubble it's like an active volcano
it can pop up in your face at any moment

so now comes the fun part!
we're gonna crush the tomatoes
pour a can of solid progresso whole plum tomatoes
with the basil leaves into a pasta strainer
then get ahold of the tomatoes with your bare hands
feel how nice'n soft'n tender those tomatoes are
they should feel like velvet
ooohh
yeah
by me crushin these tomatoes with my hands
knocks off two hours of boiling
this way you never get that friggin spotty sauce
with all the lumps
go like this
swish
　　swish
　　　　swish

nicky d's famous marinara sauce

make sure you get all the juices out
then squeeze TIGHT
squeeze TIGHT
then you push in here
push
    push
        push
            push

mmmmm
there's nothin like crushin tomatoes with your bare hands
what fun!

now take the can and fill it up halfway with some water
(don't waste nothin
next you're gonna use it as a holder)

now . . .
with the gas still low
blend your paste and the toasted garlic with your tomatoes
pour in the water and blend with the spoon
see how smooth it is?
if you threw the whole can in without crushin
you'd be here two weeks waitin for it to cook

now . . .
before we cover the pot let's put our spices in
put some salt in
(you can put in as much salt as you like
cause it evaporates in with the sauce)
a coupla pinches of black pepper
throw in some more basil
and then you gotta crush the fennel
take out your seed smasher
put some seeds in there
and CRUSH
  CRUSH
     CRUSH
       CRUSH
by doin this you build power from your gut to your biceps
pulverizing seeds builds strength
rub em up against the sides
open em
    break em
      open em
        break em
     and then you CRUSH
        open
      break
then you CRUSH

feel yourself **breakin em**
that's what you wanna do
break em

when the fennel's nice'n smooth
open up the lid and pour it in with the rest of your spices
blend it
  blend
    blend
      blend
        blend

when it comes to a vigorous boil
give it a coupla turns
then cut it down to a simmer
and keep the lid closed tight

if you want your sauce thick
you can crack the lid a little
if you want your sauce loose
keep the lid shut down
after a half hour it's all done

my sauce is blended so you can drink it like juice
if you wanna know what the secret ingredient is
i'll tell you the secret
it's not the garlic
it's not the basil
it's not the salt'n pepper

crushed fennel seed

that's the secret ingredient
it offsets the bellyaches
the sicilians never figured that out
  that's why they all walk around with *agitta*
    all the years i been makin that sauce
      nobody
          nobody
              nobody ever had a problem with gas

nicky d.'s famous pizza pie

PRODUCE OF U.S.A. *Ingredients*

globs of pizza dough
nicky d.'s famous marinara sauce
oregano
mozzarella cheese
fresh parsley
(grated) parmesan or ricotta
salt'n pepper

first i go and buy globs of pizza dough
already risen
a half a dozen globs is enough for six pizza pies

the main thing in pizza
you always gotta remember this:
(i don't give a shit if you're greek or jewish or from mars
anybody can make pizza)
the main thing in pizza is
people gotta like it!
and what makes em like it?
it's not the dough
it's not the cheese
it's not the oregano

it's the sauce!

it's the sauce that makes or breaks a pizza
the cheese and the crust everywhere you go
order a slice of pizza
it's all the same thing
it's the sauce that makes the difference!

but who's gonna take the time to make a great sauce?
the local pizza place down the block?
f'get about it!
the sauce i just showed you
i make for me and you and whatever gang i got

you can't make that commercially
you'll go broke!
all they do is buy these big gallon cans of tomatoes
dump it in a big vat
put salt'n pepper in
pour it on the dough
shove it in the oven
and charge you an arm and a leg

i do my pizza sauce pretty much
the same way i make my marinara sauce
only difference is i use oregano
you don't put oregano in anything other than pizza sauce
normally i stay away from all them stinky spices
(oregano . . . black pepper . . . cinnamon)
they're all killers of the human race
that's why after you leave a party
three hours later you're home sick with a bellyache
but in pizza you got no choice
you gotta put oregano in pizza!
blend it in with your sauce
and let it simmer all together on the stove

while that's cookin
you got time to work your dough
Flip it
put it in a nice flat pan
then with your two fingers make indentations
into the edges of the dough
all the while spinnin the pan round'n round
                    spin the pan
                        spin the pan
                            spin the pan
make sure it's THIN like paper in the middle
and the crust is heavy out towards the edges
otherwise you don't got no crust
besides the crust
THIN is the trick
    THIN
        THIN THIN
            THIN

that heavy **thick** sicilian dough

they throw all that yeast in there so it pops up like a couch
it sticks to your ribs
to your intestines
just take a piece of that fuckin goo
roll it up and FLING it against the wall
i guarantee it'll stick there

nicky d.'s famous pizza pie

and all the cheese they put on it
it's gummy and shlooey
and that sauce they put on it
when you bite into it you get that burnin acidy tang
no good no good

now it's time to take the sauce and ring it around
  spin the pan
      round and round
         and round
get out your mozzarell
cut it in skinny strips on the cutting board

      lay it all around
    round and round
cut some more strips

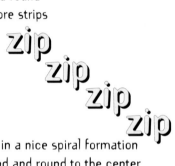

        in a nice spiral formation
      round and round to the center
    till your pie is completely covered
  (don't put the strips of mozzarell too close together
cause once it's in the oven it blends and melts)
then season it with some fresh parsley if you want
all around
   all around
      the salt'n pepper
     all around
then throw the parmesan or ricotta cheese on top of that
then more sauce on top of that
spin your pan round and round
make sure to wet the crust with tomato
tomato the crust till it's nice and wet
otherwise it'll be as hard as a rock
and you don't want your crust to burn
cause people love to eat good crust

these days alotta people put broccoli on top
mushrooms and onions and peppers
all kinds of junk

the only pizza i like is mozzarell — straight!
all that other stuff makes me sick
how can you enjoy pizza with all of that crap on top?
if you wanna eat all that shit
why don't you just cook yourself a hero
when you wanna eat pizza

you wanna eat pizza!
pizza is dough and cheese and sauce
that's pizza!
anything else is a stew or a casserole
i'd like to find out who started that new concoction
that's not pizza

so when you got all that prepared
you just **zip**
it into the oven at 350°
flip the light on so you can look inside
sit back and watch the show
watch how it bubbles up nice
then after about fifteen minutes
watch for the ridge
when it gets golden brown
get one of them flip things
lift it up and see if it's ready
you don't wanna take it out too early or too late
cause that crust has got to be perfect
i seen people just eat the crust on my pizza
they can't believe it
most people only know pizza that's just gooey and doughy
not my pizza
my pizza is edible right through to the middle
it ain't soggy
it ain't heavy
as soon as you put it on the table
they wipe it all out (my pizza)
the hot dogs and the barbecued chicken
and all that other stuff
they leave behind

pasta'n meatballs

Ingredients

> pure chuck (fresh ground)
> stale italian bread
> nicky d.'s famous marinara sauce
> olive oil (100% virgin)
> garlic (bunch of cloves)
> basil (fresh if you got it)
> parsley (if you can get it fresh)
> salt'n pepper
> eggs (grade A)

first get nicky d.'s famous marinara sauce goin
on the stove
then open up all your spices
before you start to make your run on the meatballs
so's you don't get chopped meat all over everything
then you're ready for the big job
the big job is the *polpette*
that's what we call meatballs — *polpette*

this morning i took my stale italian bread
(every time i get italian bread
i throw the heels in the vegetable bin and save em)
i put the bread in a bowl of water
so it could soak for a coupla hours (maybe half a day)
till it's nice'n soft

some people make meatballs hard as a rock
cause they don't bread it or they use bread crumbs
i never use bread crumbs
unless i'm stuck with no italian bread

now . . .
sink your bare hands into the soaking bread
compress the bread in the water
 and press it down
   press it down
     press it down
       keep pressin it

till it gets nice and tight
if you ain't got no italian bread
you can throw four or five slices of white bread
in there instead

now put your chuck in a big bowl
and open it up
open up the chuck
   squeeze it right through your fingers
    squeeze it
      squeeze it
most people don't wanna mix it like i mix
you gotta have strong hands to do this job

now . . .
cut up some fresh garlic off the fingernail just like before
CHOP
      CHOP
          CHOP
get it as small as possible so when you're cookin it
the garlic dissipates right into the meat
some people make meatballs

when you bite down
you're bitin on
a big chunk of garlic
no good no good!
it burns your mouth

you gotta have patience when you chop garlic
help the flame
help the stove
help the meatballs
help the taste
help the intestines
help the garlic to dissipate faster
by choppin that garlic
as small as you can

nicole got one of them food processors
i'll never use it
she says
        use the choppa nicky!
   i say
        no i don't wanna use that
        i use my knife and my hands
        that's all i need

pasta 'n meatballs

i do everything with this knife
this knife can tell you stories
my mother used to use this knife
it's my favorite
i been sharpenin this beauty for fifty years

now . . .
put a little drop of salt over the chopped meat
and the raw garlic
add a little pepper
then a little fresh parsley
that's all you need
sicilians put pignoli nuts in their *polpette*
but i don't want no interference
when i'm bitin on them juicy soft meatballs

resume mixin with your fingers
like you're a grinder in a butcher shop
blend it all into the raw meat
KNEADIN the meat
  KNEAD IT
    KNEAD IT

now . . .
go get the soaking bread
squeeze out as much water as possible
    squeeze
        squeeze
PRESS into it with your palms
  PRESS
      PRESS
          PRESS
              PRESS
squeeze
break it down as much as possible
cause you want your meatballs soft

make sure you keep checkin your sauce
give it a nice toss
blend it blend it

now . . .
bring your bread over to the table
and put it in another bowl
(always make sure you're in a place
that has good maneuverability)
don't feel like you hafta use all the bread
cause you don't wanna end up with bread balls
you're makin meatballs!

you can always make a nice *naplidan* cake
with the bread you got left over

now comes the big operation:
you gotta be like a surgical technician on this
take an egg

crack it
DROP IT

take another egg

crack it
DROP IT

take another egg

crack it
DROP IT

no broken shells
you want nothin but egg in there
the best way to crack an egg is with one sharp rap
my mother always taught me
after you crack an egg
you gotta put the eggshells in paper
and crush em with your hands
only after that can you throw em away
never throw an eggshell away
without crushin it first
it's some kind of hand-me-down thing from the old country
it shows supremacy over the things of the world
even when somebody else is cookin
if i see them leave the eggshells over
i go and flatten em down

i learnt about alotta things from watchin my mom cook
but i also made improvements along the way
cause she used alotta pork in her cooking
alotta spareribs and sausages
and skin backs
her sauces were good but they were greasy
i don't do that
my sauces are pure!

okay . . .
right now the bread is bland
so let's add salt to the bread and eggs
the bread needs alotta salt
you can't mix the bread with the meat and then add eggs
each operation's gotta be done separate
otherwise the meat will interfere with the eggs

pasta'n meatballs

get your hands in there and blend
and blend it
KNEAD the egg right into the bread
blend it
  blend it
    mix it up with the bread
      till the bread's soaked through and through with egg
you gotta use your hands on this too
no cheatin!
squeeze
   squeeze
     slow
       slow
         blend it
           slow slow
        blend it
      squeeze
    blend it
  blend it
now look how nice and moist it's startin to get
after so many years
you can feel when it starts to be the right consistency
(when i go out to long island
we got no jews there
so i can also put in some parmesan cheese at this point
if there are jews around
then you should skip the parmesan)
keep blendin it till it starts to feel
a little like pizza dough
no lumps
no big chunks
no disruptions

there's a recipe in the newspaper today
by rita and ronnie that's disgusting!
they're tellin you to put things in there that fight each other
they tell you to put diced up onions in with the garlic
never put onions
and garlic together
in the same meal
cause they cancel
each other out!
you never know who's gonna win the battle
the onion or the garlic

how the hell
can you taste both
at the same time?
it's impossible

rita and ronnie also tell you to throw in bell peppers
how can you even mention
bell pepper and onion in the same breath?
the irish do that
i don't understand how they can do that
that's gonna give you *agitta* f'sure

they also put three bay leaves in there
bay leaves and basil
cancel each other out!
they also say to put
oregano in meatballs
now that's the worst of all
oregano will wipe out any kind of thing you put in there
it'll even wipe out the garlic
don't eat spices
eat food!
salt'n pepper are the only spices i know
(basil by the way is not a spice
you could eat a basil salad with oil'n vinegar)

want me to prove how bad spices are?

get a tablespoon of black pepper
and put it in your gas tank
then you have to throw your car away
now if it does that to your car
think about what it does to your kidneys
the way i use spices
you don't taste it
everything blends in even

now . . .
take out your skillet for the meatballs
make sure you use a good cast-iron or copper skillet
somethin that'll cook your balls
nice and even all around

pasta'n meatballs

if you wanna know the secret to makin great meatballs
it's not the size of the ball
it's not the eggs
it's not the bread
the real secret to meatballs is

fresh ground chuck

just add olive oil to keep it from stickin on you
don't worry about the olive oil neither
you can drink good olive oil straight if you want
there's no cholesterol
it's actually healthy for your intestines
me and my brother vinny
when we were teenagers
we used to comb out our hair with olive oil

don't forget to check the sauce
give it a little spin
spin it spin it
i don't taste it or nothin
i never hafta taste what i'm cookin!
i let other people taste
(my brother always sticks a piece of italian bread in there
while it's still on the stove
he's my taster)

so now it's time to roll up the balls
so they're nice and round
start with the palms
roll em up to the fingers in a nice rotation
roll with your right hand and pivot against the left
see how nice and soft and flexible they are?
i like em small
there's no one size that's right
gina and nicole and all of them make em twice that size

the way the *polpette* go into the skillet
is the way they're gonna come out
only smaller
when you roll out a dozen or so
and you got a ten-inch skillet
then you put em in all at once
don't put em in as you make em
put the lid on so you cook em on both sides
then you just flip em to get the golden color
as dark as you want

FLIP
  FLIP
    FLIP
      FLIP
        FLIP

while they're cookin
roll up another dozen
then put up a pot of water and pick out a spaghetti
any variety you like

      thick

       skinny

      long

        screws

       ziti

        fusilli

        linguini

        rotelli

        elbows

         bow ties

you can pick whatever you like
but don't ever mix pastas
cause they each have different cookin times
you'll ruin your whole friggin meal!

i don't know what the hell rita and ronnie are talkin about
they say to pour oil into the pot when you cook pasta
my pasta never sticks!

the lazy bastards
just dump it in
and walk away

no wonder their pasta sticks together
i'm continuously *STIRRIN* with a big stirrin spoon
  STIRRIN
 STIRRIN
  STIRRIN

maybe make the second batch more well done
so you got a variety
when the bottom gets dark
that's when they rake em off right outta the pan
wherever i go they eat my meatballs
before they ever get a chance to
mix in with the sauce
i get so mad sometimes
by the time it's time to serve dinner

pasta'n meatballs

everybody says

hey . . .
where's the
meatballs?

wait till you smell em
you'll go berserk

when i was a kid
we used to come home from mass on sundees
and see a bowl of these on the stove
we'd wipe em out right on the stove
my mother had to make two times the amount i do

i usually make my sauces about eleven o'clock
on a sundee morning
so i can eat by 2:30
it'll taste good if you take it off the stove right away
but in three or four hours
it'll taste even better
it blends in more
cause it has time to ferment
and tomorrow
it'll taste even better!

to serve:
drain the pasta
put some on each plate
top it with the sauce
then put the bowl of *polpette* on the table
and let people go at it however they want
(some people mix the meatballs in with the pot of sauce
and let it cook together
but i keep it separate
cause the second you put those balls on a plate
with the sauce
they open right up
they absorb into the sauce
by the time they break in your mouth
they're like velvet
mmmmmmm

i see how alotta young people today
don't know how to eat meatballs
you wanna know how to eat these things
you go like this
(let em cool off)
then just pop a meatball in your mouth
two bites and down

these things're killers
nobody can stop from eatin em
on top of that they're the best things for you
you can throw all your pills away
all your vitamins
everything in these meatballs is medicine
garlic keeps all the vampires away
 salt'n pepper keeps the blood circulatin
   and the chuck keeps the beast alive inside you
   all of it is good
          if you keep eatin these meatballs
                 you'll be alright
                    yeah

pasta fagioli (quicky version)

PRODUCE OF U.S.A. *Ingredients*

tomato sauce (del monte)
garlic
basil
fennel
salt'n pepper
no meat (unless you want it)
chickpeas or cannellini beans
your favorite kind of pasta

if you got any neurotic vegetarians comin over for dinner
this is a quick meatless thing to make

after ten years of bein a vegetarian
warren finally broke down and ate some nice pure chuck
i made him some of my famous meatballs
he couldn't resist
it made him healthy for one day
gave him some real protein for a change
put some red back in his cheeks

but now he's gone right back to the same old routine
with the veggie burgers and tofu
there's somethin wrong with him
what's he scared of?
he's scared of somethin
he's afraid of eatin a well-cooked hamburger
he's afraid of eatin a roast beef sandwich
actually my nice meatballs probably didn't do him any good
cause he ate it with fear
he ate them meatballs
with fear

look at him
he's got no good color in his face
he's got no energy
he's a leaf-eatin vegetarian!

there's all kinds of ways of makin pasta fagioli
my favorite is with elbow macaroni and cannellini beans
what you do is
heat up some olive oil in the skillet
chop up some garlic and toast it golden brown
if you don't have the time to make the marinara sauce
just open up a can of del monte tomato sauce
and add all the same spices i put in the marinara

your sauce'll be all done in twenty minutes
put it down to a very low simmer
open up your can of cannellini beans
or you can use chickpeas if you like that better
drain it and throw the chickpeas in your sauce
then let it simmer another ten fifteen minutes
shut it off

when you're ready to eat
boil up a pot of water
then throw in any kind of macs you want
even spaghetti
just remember to break the spaghetti three times
if you're gonna eat with a spoon
if you're thinkin of eatin it with a fork
then you got a problem
cause you got chickpeas in there
and chickpeas hafta be scooped up with a spoon
that's why you're better off usin pastina or elbows

when your pasta is ready
take the tomato sauce and put it on top of the pasta
SQUISH it around
   SQUISH it around
       SQUISH SQUISH SQUISH

within a half hour you got yourself a meatless meal

if you're eatin alone
or you don't got any vegetarians comin over
you can also put things in like a coupla frankfurters
slice em up and saute em a little
mix it in with the pasta fagioli

now isn't that delicious?

recipe for sleep

PRODUCE OF U.S.A.   *Ingredients*

| caramel covered pecans

what i do to go to sleep is
eleven o'clock at night
star trek comes on
i lock the door
(don't let nobody in)
i open up a box of caramel covered pecans
lay back in my couch
and one by one
i eat the whole box in half an hour

after eatin all that
i'm gone
i fall right off to sleep
like a baby
 t.v. blaring
   bombs goin off
      it doesn't matter
         nothin in the world can rattle me
            nothin

This book was printed by offset lithography on acid-free paper. All prepress work was composed by Warren Lehrer on Macintosh computers using Adobe Photoshop, Aldus PageMaker, Quark Express, Aldus Freehand, and TypeStyler. The primary type family used for the voice of Nicky D. is Template, a Barry Deck design, published by Emigre. ITC Clearface is the principal text face used for the introductory and back-matter pages. Over two dozen other typefaces are used throughout the book as well. The photograph of Marilyn Monroe by Philippe Halsman, © Halsman Estate, is reprinted courtesy of the Halsman Estate.

Many, many thanks to

my wife, Judith Sloan, for her encouragement, assistance, and wisdom; my editors, Sharon Dahl and Patricia Draher, for their tireless insight and care; Sally Brunsman, Kim Barnett, Philip Kovacevich, Sharon Rose Vonasch, and all the people at Bay Press for believing in me and making this implausible project a reality; my agent, Donald Farber, for separating good from evil spirits; and the New York State Council on the Arts, New York State Foundation for the Arts, and the Purchase College Association for their financial support. Also, special thanks to Jim Frank, Joan Lyons and the Visual Studies Workshop, Frank and Toni DiTommaso, Ruth and Arthur Lehrer, Leonard Seastone, Vicki Dennis, Brian Lehrer, Clifton Meador, Margot Lovejoy, Phil Zimmermann, Lesley Stone, Rod Richardson, and Brad Freeman for all their help. Most of all, I want to thank Nicky D. for being himself.

Warren Lehrer

is a writer, artist, performer, and book designer who celebrates the music of thought and speech, the complexity of personality, and the fine line between humor and tragedy. Acclaimed as "one of the most imaginative book artists of our time," Lehrer is known as a pioneer in the burgeoning field of visual literature. His previous books include *GRRRHHHH: a study of social patterns*, *FRENCH FRIES, i mean you know*, and *versations*. Lehrer's plays include *The Basic Training of Eugene Solomon*, cowritten with Dennis Bernstein, and *Denial of the Fittest* and *A Tattle Tale*, cowritten with his wife, Judith Sloan. Lehrer and Sloan also coproduced the weekly satirical radio segment *The Whole K'Cuffin World Report* for Pacifica Radio. With Harvey Goldman, Lehrer composed a contemporary opera entitled *The Search for IT and Other Pronouns*. His books have been exhibited internationally and are in the collections of major museums. He has received grants from the National Endowment for the Arts, the New York State Council on the Arts, the New York State Foundation for the Arts, and the Ford Foundation as well as numerous awards, including three American Institute for Graphic Arts Book Awards and the International Book Design Award. Lehrer lives in New York City and teaches at the State University of New York at Purchase. He is presently working on **The Portrait Series** books based on women.